Momifesto

A Manifesto of 9 Practices for Phenomenal Moms

Vikki Spencer, M.Ed.

Dedication

To the great-greats and grandmothers influencing this book in unseen but powerful ways, I dedicate this to you...

The late Grandmothers: Mary Gilbert, Ewdokia Bojarski

Grandmother Anne Hardin, "Grammy" and stepmom, Leslie

My mother, Marlene, who modeled faith, the high road, and how to graciously accept every stage of life with me and my sister, Cindy. I love you.

And to my son, Jordan. Out of all the moms in the world how did I get so lucky to be YOUR mom? I love who you were, who you are, and who you will be. One day may you understand the force you were to help me grow and heal.

HOLD ON MOM!

Before you go any further, don't forget to pick up your free gift!

As a thank you for buying the book, you can pick up a free copy of the workbook "*Momifesto: 9 DIY Practices for Moms*"

Click here now!

Or visit: http://themomwhisperer.com/momifesto/

Acknowledgements

There is a dream team of expertise behind every stage of this book!

From concept to completion, I want to acknowledge the excellence of Karen Salmansohn, Lorraine Ketch, Jessica Gang, Mama Red Knight, and Lise Cartwright.

Special thanks to Brendon Burchard, Marie Forleo, Brene Brown, Marcus Buckingham, Diane Gross, Ike Patterson, Melody Ross, Maya Rachel Stein, Hannah Marcotti, Leslie B. and Cindy B.

Mitch Matthews for keeping dreams alive amidst crisis, and knowing the next step in business before I knew to ask.

Kevin Spencer for supporting the choice for me to be home with Jordan so we could get this right. Thank you for that gift.

My friends, near and far, who are unafraid of authenticity, crisis, and impossible optimism. You gave when I had nothing to give. Apparently, you are stuck with me: Leslie W., Sharon S., Erika N., Kerri M., Jen W., and Jen T., Kathryn P., Kathy S. and Mary S.

Table of Contents

CHAPTER 1
Introduction

Need Help?
You're Not Crazy. This Book is For You!

Whether it's the brilliant women who find me for coaching, or my beautiful friends, or amazing women I overhear in public, they all believe in more—for their families and their lives.

We've been told as young women to dream, build a life, choose well, and be happy (no pressure).

But now there are kids—and they refuse to let go of the hope for more. They become warriors for their family in the most heroic ways possible.

They want the map—the one designed especially for us, especially for each kid.

They skim parenting books then toss them, unable to figure out which chapter they're supposed to read first.

They look at what they're surrounded by and are a little freaked out at the tasks ahead.

They don't ask friends any more because they are trekking too, and they don't know either.

They know they are at a standstill but don't know which direction to start.

Ultimately, they say, "I don't know what else to do. Please fix it." Maybe it's parenting. They want to make their toddler/ tween/ teen stop/ change/ listen.

They are burning the candle at both ends— staying up late and getting up early, and they are exhausted from doing it all. They don't know who they are, don't have time for anything, and would like the hallway closet—if not the whole house—decluttered.

Typically, the only piece of advice they hear is "put on your oxygen mask."

If I could change one thing in the entire mom world, it would be a ban on the oxygen mask advice (usually given by well meaning individuals without children at home). It goes like this: You have to take care of yourself first. When you're on an airplane, they always say put your own mask on before you help your child.

Life is like that—take care of yourself first.

I call BS on that whole, entire analogy.

We are not seated in a plane.

Our kids are not buckled in and immobile while we are served a selection of beverages.

We are not reading a magazine.

We are not inhaling and exhaling through a yellow mask, or taking a quick nap because our kid is watching an entire 90-minute movie on an iPad while buckled in, drinking juice and eating pretzels.

We are not sitting peacefully next to our tween and/or teen, talking about what snacks they want when someone else is delivering them.

We are not admitting it, but we are locating the

nearest exit, fantasizing about popping open the door, and parachuting out. It doesn't matter where we land.

We could not afford to be tethered to an oxygen mask because there is no one else to pour soda or find extra pretzels out of thin air while all the lights are being pushed like flashes of lightning during a storm.

We are shutting off smoke alarms, resetting call buttons, and taking care of overflowing toilets... On both ends of the plane.

We are the only stewardesses on the plane.

For every flight.

We are also the pilot navigating where we go, how fast, and when the whole thing lands. We are very aware that every day is a new flight in uncharted territory and we are on "sight only" because there is no map.

Fog every single day.

We have already deployed every oxygen mask on the flight. We want everyone to stop and breathe, and buckle themselves in. We are trying to think — quickly.

AND we are the cleaning crew getting things ready for the next day, stocking sodas, replacing magazines, vacuuming, and cleaning toilets.

Let me ask you this: Does it sound like an oxygen mask is going to cut it?

Not even close.

But it's even worse than that...

We don't need an oxygen mask; we need a very mobile oxygen tank because we're not on a plane at all.

Motherhood could not be reduced to a plane ride on the best days. As a long-term commitment, full of unimaginable awe and breathtaking pain, the commitment to the journey is much more epic than a plane flight.

Every mom is actually journeying her own Mt. Everest. This is the symbolic journey we find ourselves on.

Lest you doubt, let me make a few comparisons.

At some point, we thought this was going to be a great idea.

We start out—ecstatic.

We train for it. We read. We ask questions.
We find we're better prepared than others.
We're not better than others.
We need a nap.
We need air.
We are numb.
We need someone to put the oxygen tank on our back and the mask on our face.
We need to feel safe.
We need to watch out for avalanches of every sort.
We are crazy.
We spend too much money.

Why we do it—because we felt "led" to do it.

The one perk we have to look forward to is once they leave the house, we tell epic tales of raising our kid(s)...

Everest alone would not even complete the

picture—add in a tough marriage, freaky in-laws, and religion and politics, and you have the mind numbing trip to the summit of motherhood.

So this is why it is the picture of Everest that I often have in my head when I'm approached for coaching. My clients feel inadequate, embarrassed, often at their end. They apologize and feel ashamed as if they should know better. They have no clue they're on Everest. But I do. I know we are all climbing.

So they sign on and I send them an intake form. It's a basic form that helps me see where the holes are, what they really want to work on, and where we can begin.

Most moms can only fill out half of it.

It's not for being ignorant, or not thoughtful, or not trying. It's that they never thought about the questions.

They knew what they didn't want—to feel overwhelmed, flailing as a parent, and not enjoying life. Nobody signs up for Everest to be miserable. We sign up for the life transformation, to prove ourselves, to have killer stories to tell our grandkids. But sometimes on the climb, we forget all that.

The intake form asks them to remember or dream or consider what they do want. In fact, I give instructions to leave nothing blank. Give me something.

Wonder how you would do?

Try it for yourself. This form can be found on www.themomwhisperer.com/intake.

Regardless of how much is filled out or not, everything they write is brilliant. The pieces they have are brilliant, the ones they don't have, equally so. There is no right or wrong, but we need the starting place—wherever it is.

From the places most filled out and the ones most often left blank, and how clients have moved toward their changes, I identified the nine places that moms overlook or don't consider and that most of the parenting books don't talk about.

I've been using these exact nine practices myself

for over 16 years. I've shared with friends, then clients, for hundreds of hours. They not only work, they allow a place for healing, focus, movement, and change—on your terms and on your family's.

They are founded in a cross-disciplinary approach—meaning they are based in business, happiness, psychology, etc. When we have answers to these questions, we have an idea of where we're going and why and the markers along the way to get there. Otherwise, we can work on making our kids behave, but they will still not have a vibrant family life that includes a mom who is engaged, and who loves and celebrates her family.

Try the intake form and see where you are strong and where you could use some information. I don't expect you to know or master every point, so don't require it of yourself. It's a guide.

What's My Chapter?

Want to know which chapter is yours?

You choose which one to start first. You see where your family rates highly and where some work would help. These concepts are offered to you in bite sized pieces that inspire shifting, tweaking, and re-thinking family.

You've already heard part of my story, but I'll continue to share my story throughout the book because I know what it's like to feel in your gut that there must be a plan but maybe I didn't show up on the day the books were handed out.

I'm also writing this book for my friends...

- The one with the three boys in 4th- 10th grade.
- The one with twins.
- The one with a toddler and a five-year-old.
- The single mom who is traveling to keep food on the table for her growing teen son.

These are my friends who have picked my brain but didn't hire me because funds were tight. Their expectation for this book: Make it simple, I don't have a lot of time.

This is for them. And it's for you.

Two Sections To Save Time

To expedite finding what you most need, you'll find two sections that help you focus more deeply.

"This is for you if..."

If you didn't even have time to fill out the intake form (HERE) to see which chapter you would most benefit from—no problem! Skim the beginnings of each chapter to find your most needed areas of help.

How will you know if it's "the one"? Because your inner voice will say, "Really? That can be fixed?" or "I so need that," or "Yes, please—yesterday."

The DIY

DIY—Do It Yourself.

This is the whole "I don't have the money to hire a coach, but I need to make changes" section. The questions are designed specifically to address the concepts in the book AND incorporating the motto into your life. In fact, some of the DIY challenges are what I've given my clients to work on between sessions.

Yes, they too are magic. ;-)

I want this book to be the go-to resource when it's all going really wrong and I want to show you ways to get climbing instead of sitting on the mountain. Sulking. With a drink or chocolate.

It's markers.
It's a path.
It's shells on the beach.
It's stones in the stream.

Whatever your journey looks like, this helps you along the way.

Your journey with personal markers that no one is talking about.

Mom gold.

My heart is that moms move past the fear, guilt, and insecurities of "Am I doing enough? Am I on track? What if I'm messing it all up?"

I imagine a world of moms who sparkle with confidence in their skills, talents, and connection with their kids (of any age), deeply grateful for the experience of family, full of relentless pride over who their kids are becoming, and humbled at the thought that they are walking in their destiny and purpose as part of a great chain of mothers and grandmothers and great grandmothers who have put us on their shoulders and carried us. Who look down on us and say in the spring breeze, and the winter frost, "We are with you. You fulfill and honor us. We bless you."

Put one foot in front of the other and look at the views along the way because this trip is really once in a lifetime, with no two days the same.

This book is your oxygen tank for the Everest-like trek of being mom. The other moms reading, our team.

The sherpa? We have one inside of us. We can call it whatever we want to, but once we tap into it, we no longer feel alone.

This book will be your new guidebook. We are roped together sharing masks, tanks, and chocolate. It will put into perspective our personal journey, gifts, wishes, and families. You will find places to stand, words for your life, and a sanity that holds things together in the darkest nights. In the mornings, you'll shift with new perspectives and feel prepared to engage in a new day, with new concepts that have been laid like tracks in snow for others to find and follow.

This book offers solid places to stand on but no guarantees. I am promising to give you the best odds of creating a phenomenal family life so regrets are minimal if any. I cannot promise a perfect life, but I can help you make strong, sure moves toward your best life—in its messy, beautiful glory so you will look back on every day and believe you did your very best.

And all you have to bring along is an open heart, truthful stories, and some chocolate.

As you are reading, I want you to remember this.

Everest is the highest mountain in the world. Oxygen masks are useless. Oxygen tanks are essential.

The locals consider it sacred, a force. They

deeply revere the symbol and force that it is. They are humbled by it. They live, work and are sustained on it. They recognize what happens to those who take on the challenge, surrender to it, and respect it.... the ones transformed.

The highest mountain in your world is not your job, your social class, your bank account, your friends, in-laws, politics, or religion. It's your family. It requires more than hyperventilating into an oxygen mask like a good girl.

It requires stamina, ferocity, and humility. It's sacred, a force.

Let it transform you.

CHAPTER 2
My Story

A long time ago in a land far away, my husband and I had a dream and two free airline tickets to go visit Colorado. We intended to move to Denver to forge a new life outside of teaching high school, a life on our own, away from the familiarity of North Carolina.

Things would be different, better.

The day before we were to leave, I went to the doctor because I had the "flu" for about two weeks. Only, I didn't have the flu. I had a baby. But we were heading to grad school, the Rockies, and distance from family.

I knew how to want that life. I didn't know how to want this one. Family WAS on the radar, but not at that moment. We were on the 10-year plan. A baby hadn't been on my radar.

Guess what else wasn't on my radar.

Government sponsored Women, Infant, Children

(WIC) lines, six straight months of morning sickness. Gaining 30 pounds when I was still trying to lose 10. Sleepless nights, bottles, diapers, crying...

All my twenty-something self wanted was Colorado. I had no clue about babies. And instead of moving away from family and getting that distance, we stayed.

During that time, I learned about post-partum depression, finding my maternal instinct, and that the best book to have in the bathroom besides What to Expect Your First Year is 7 Habits of Highly Effective People. That book taught me that not only did I need an assistant, but I needed a vision, and that I was the chicken that took care of the golden egg... our son, Jordan.

I told myself that as soon as the sleep deprivation wore off, I would take care of both.

Seriously, I did...

I began dreaming and visioning and taking one night a week off from being Mom. I read about how babies' brains develop the first year and interacted with my son in ways other moms didn't.

Taking criticism for choices that made sense to me, all I knew for sure was that in 13 years we'd have a teen to deal with and in many ways, the beginnings of that started the first year.

Needless to say, stress, arguing, and crisis quickly wore out the welcome mat of my marriage. I remember taking my 6-month-old to the first of many hours of my own counseling visits.

Maybe it was 18,000 hours total, but who's counting...

What started to become clear in those sessions was the need for me to address past childhood hurts, so that my "mom style" would not be born from my own lack of experience, but instead a conscious, thinking, if not well intended, struggle for authenticity and love.

By age three, Jordan was in preschool and within a few years I started going to writer's conferences because I wanted to write a book. I hired a coach to help me uncover my passion, purpose, strengths, values, and vision. This revolutionized how I saw myself, allowing me to leverage positive, strong, and beautiful traits that helped ease the guilt and fear of not being enough in the world.

Apparently, my visionary, logical, hopeful side caught the attention of a local radio station that hired me as a part-time on-air morning show co-host.

Life seemed to find a rhythm that served everyone...

...Until it didn't.

Within four weeks of my going back to work part-time, we were notified by our sons' teachers that some of his actions felt "off" and they suggested we speak with his doctor. After a visit to the pediatrician, Jordan was diagnosed with Obsessive Compulsive Disorder (OCD) and Tourette's tics.

For the year of Kindergarten, my day started at 3:30am, changing wet bed sheets from an anxious little heart, and by 4:30am leaving for work. I came home at 11:00am, picked Jordan up at noon, and we ate lunch. Often our days consisted of us finding another doctor to try—psychologist, psychiatrist, homeopathic, naturopathic, chiropractic, nutritionist, therapist, food allergy shots—and waiting 4-6 weeks to see if the new treatment "worked." I didn't want to waste more time waiting with no cure, but I believed that my 6-year-old could be helped, because a child's brain is still forming.

During this time, we ate a lot of breakfasts for dinner so we could budget for the doctors. We didn't argue about money, though. We argued about everything else and couldn't hide that chaos from our son.

Sometimes all the medicine in the world can't fix what a child feels is going on around him.

At the time, I was part of a Bible study group and asked them to pray for us. A woman in the group steered us to Duke University, where they were doing a research study on pediatric OCD. The university gave us 12 PhD candidates and professors who could help us decide if Jordan's case was anxiety or physically based, and then provide the best therapy they had available.

When we initially went into the study, I began by saying it was all my fault—it was my parenting, my ineptness, I missed signs, our marriage was tough, that I would do anything necessary to help him get better. Tai, our assigned PhD candidate asked me why I believed this. "Because his tics and symptoms are awful when I'm around and not so bad when everyone else is. I cause them because I don't know what I'm doing."

She said, "It's always the mother's fault."

It is?

Tai said, "I'm kidding. Moms are just easiest to blame. Truth is, there are a LOT of factors that go into this. But what you need to know is that Jordan's symptoms are worse around you, because he's comfortable to do them around you. He tries to hold it in with everyone else and releases it at the end of the school day with you.

We are going to need you to help him in the ways we ask. You also need to know that with one special needs child in the house, there is usually a 96% divorce rate."

I was reeling. She said "special needs," and "divorce," yet I was relieved to learn that I was not the sole reason all this was happening.

The study helped us find new ways of dealing with Jordan's tics, with him hoarding 61 paper airplanes, with our parenting, and with helping to retrain thoughts and learning to refocus.

The collective team landed on a split decision: six believing anxiety was a cause, and six believing it was a physical cause.

So, I went against their recommendation and homeschooled Jordan in second grade so we could have more control over his environment and really learn what he most needed from spending time together.

We shifted everything. We crafted a multi-dimensional plan that included removing food allergens, providing supplements for things he was deficient in, encouraging exercise on a trampoline, playing with the neighborhood kids, etc.

In the middle of this overwhelming time, one late night after surfing the web for more information, I was exhausted, tapped out, and praying.

What about me?

I wanted a coach, a Mom whisperer, someone who identified and understood my strengths as a mom, not as a writer or on-air personality. I wanted someone to look at the visionary, logical, hopeful person I was earlier in my life and help me leverage it all for the homeschooling and marital situation.

I was tired of feeling as if it was nearly impossible most days, battling depression, fear, and guilt. Where was the good? Where did this make sense? How is this okay? Because I was very convinced on some level, I was made for this situation and family.

Wanting to believe that someone could help me, I searched online for "Mom Whisperer" but there was none. That particular .com was available though, and I figured one day I might be able to sell it, so I bought it.

Within a year of homeschooling, Jordan was nearly symptom free and went back to school for third grade. My husband and I gave in to the pressure of the tumult that was our family and separated.

During this time, everyone was in therapy for something.

After only a six-month separation, my husband and I reconciled and took a dream vacation, surfed in Hawaii, and through weird circumstances, moved four times within three years.

Jordan's OCD and Tourette's almost never reared their heads again and were kept at bay through supplements, boundaries on our time, food choices, and Jordan's own personal thoughts working for him instead of against him.

Success followed us with each of our moves. We had not just one, but two packaging businesses —sales booming, accounts flying, OCD and Tourette's nearly gone forever.

Full-time, I was running one business while my husband landed on the sales team for another. On the side, I started writing articles and ideas for other mom blogs as "The Mom Whisperer." A church hired me to coach other moms who were in counseling and needed to process and sort their lives out. Some had special needs kids, others had difficult marriages, and all of them had difficult circumstances. I taught several classes on communication and relationships, and spoke at a mom retreat.

Marriage counseling, personal therapy, and all the tricks of nutrition stayed in play for years. However, my marriage continued to unravel and we divorced. Ultimately, I learned that for sure, no family is without conflict. Everyone needs extra care, starting with ourselves, especially as moms.

We need more to hang our hats on than hugs from our family, the promise of ever after, or believing the kids will never leave our home. We need something that we can tailor to who we are made to be, regardless of the cards we play or get dealt.

The practices in this book are not just client tested, and mom approved, they are the beginning principles of a mom's life well lived— whether in WIC lines or with stuffed bank accounts. Each chapter offers a concept but never requires a particular way of doing it as "right" or "wrong." Instead, it is an opportunity to live authentically in the midst of the intensity of family life. Everything is geared toward moms —whether they are married or single, working or at home.

All nine are not required to be phenomenal. Just trying and really grounding in ONE, totally counts. You're in!

It's a platform for parenting that can unite us instead of leaving us isolated any further, with fingers pointing at us in addition to our own.

This book comes from an honest questioning of what it means to grow into being a phenomenal mom. So many well-intended books fall short because we all have our own strengths, situations, and relationships. There is no "one size fits all" advice. I'm sharing what I believe to be important—what moms are not talking about and what we might consider important enough to start talking about.

By addressing a few core concepts, we not only change the face of motherhood, but we engage in our lives and our families in revolutionary ways of love, sanity, and wisdom—phenomenal motherhood.

CHAPTER 3
Practice #1: We Require Our Sanity

For you if you need to:

- Find permission to surrender guilt, and not feel scattered anymore
- Figure out self-care
- Find a way to stop feeling crazy most days

Moms want to figure out how to make their kids listen to them, or how to de-clutter their closet, or how to change jobs. The brilliant, capable, savvy women who find me, initially ask for help in all these areas.

They may call me because they truly have no clue how to release stress—although they can Google that, they literally get lost in all the endless options.

Sometimes they call because they cannot get the "out-of-the-door" morning routine together.

They may need a resume tweaked, or a plan for a new job.

But really, at the heart of it, they find me because they don't know who they are any more and they are determined to be amazing moms in the midst of their own struggle, stress, and crises.

When a woman becomes a mom, she can lose sight of who she is. Her self concept gets stuck somewhere between who she was before pregnancy and the never-ending loads of laundry.

She is giving from an empty cup.

And when she gives from an empty cup, there is only one of four things that will happen:

- She will get depressed.
- She will get angry.
- She will get sick.
- She will leave.

I ask you ... when you're depressed, angry, sick, or want to leave, do you really need someone to help you clean your closets? Will perfect kids keep you home? Will a new job fill an empty cup?

We have to understand that the control, nitpicking, nagging, and yelling are all symptoms of a larger discontent in crisis. We need to listen to discontent. It's teaching us. It's breathing into us. It's trying to get us on track.

When my son was three months old, the apartment door opened at 6:25pm and I greeted my husband with no smile, no hug, not even a warm dinner. He was greeted with, "Do you know what they did to the Branch Davidian people in Waco, Texas? They played music all hours of the night. They wore them down in order to make them surrender. Do you realize that's what's going on here? I'm being worn down to surrender. Between the constant music downstairs and the crying every two hours, it's like warfare."

He said, "He's a baby. It's not warfare."

I said, "It's wearing me down." And promptly burst into tears.

Welcome to motherhood.

It feels different to each of us—some find their groove that first year, others find it more like, ahem ... warfare.

When our children are born, they depend on us for their very lives. We willingly accept the responsibility and sacrifice our lives, as we know it, to keep them alive.

That first year, we feel our lives shift drastically as we navigate life choices at work, home, and marriage, all while keeping alive a newborn. Some of us feel like our world shrinks into the tiny package of our child. They consume us; they are literally running every moment of our lives.

Husbands, partners, and lovers are jealous—as they should be. They have never had that much influence over every minute of our lives, and most likely, for many of them, it will be 18 years or more before we can connect again, without interruption, for longer than a 90 minute date.

During years two through five, our lives change even more. Time feels very slow. Older people in the stores offer unsolicited encouragement: "Oh, the days are long but the years are short," and "Oh, enjoy this age." While all we want to do is ask them to take our child(ren) until they are 10 and we'll come back for them then.

Often we make mental notes of what we want to do again "one day," but that one-day never seems to come. Crises, conflicts, and never-ending laundry take up most of our time. We carve a family culture out of busyness and guilt.

Once our children slip into ages six through 10, our lives open up again as we are no longer needed for the intensity of the younger years. When children go to school, we shift into work mode, often without taking stock of current interests, goals, or values.

Many moms attempt to pick up where they left off before children and they find it rarely fits them now. We ask: "What about me?" but don't have our own answer. We don't take time to listen for it, and are not quite sure we'd even recognize it if we heard it. It becomes easier to stay focused on home life.

The 'tween years are a balance of training and investing—a different way than just through modeling and correction. These are the years our children begin revealing pre-adult personalities, and conflicts are abundant.

We fail at connection, as it defies comprehension of even knowing who is now under our roof. Our time for ourselves, while possible, is tossed out the window because of our exhaustion from the mental gymnastics of family life. This age also begins the lessons, team sports, and band practices that chew away at free moments.

The teen years find us eyeing the day when they leave (for good or bad) and this is the beginning of serious calculations: Who am I without my kids when the past 15 years have been all about them? Dear God, please tell me I did enough...

If we don't feel we did enough, we try to correct, sermonize, and give lessons. Our influence in their lives is winding down, yet our own life seems to still be elusive.

It's not difficult to see why self-care, and the sanity that comes with it, is not on the radar until the very later years of a child's life. While often it's a time and energy issue, it's also a money issue. The shift to having a family and creating a life often demands our responses at break-neck speed. And, no pressure, but one wrong choice, decision, or call, and they will either be in the emergency room with a broken arm (Maybe I shouldn't have said yes to football), or the therapist's office (This is all my fault).

And don't forget about the early morning sweats—when fear feels like truth, and we worry that we really are not enough and believe that we have no clue what we're doing, and wonder, Who thought that we would be able to bring children into the world anyway?

Our life goes into our family and home. This is a daily choice. No one would say we regret it. We do not. However, we live with a teeny tiny voice that asks in the depths of our being: What about me?

Even if we can answer that tiny voice, the hurdle of skillfully inserting our own wishes into the demands of family often feels selfish: How can I ask for a night off when he's been working all day too?

So, we volunteer, because at least then, we're not selfish. If we're women of faith, we feel a bit justified: Look, we're helping others. We're serving God. We're on board to change our corner of the world.

But I don't see it that way.

Very often, when I hear of moms volunteering but not "having time" for themselves, I honor their willingness to serve but feel they are avoiding finding their own life.

My litmus test to clients?

I ask, "So, does it recharge you? Is it what you're made to do?" The answer is always negative. In fact, the one activity where they intended well, wanted to serve and make their life matter, becomes one of the hinges of their undoing. Their passion, purpose, or gifts stay on the sidelines. Often they don't even love the cause they are behind. They just wanted to matter, have others smile at them, be part of something they aren't in charge of.

As well intentioned as we are, we will never matter in the world until we find how deeply we matter to ourselves.

Underestimating the Power of Sanity, Joy, and Self-Care

Life isn't about how old the kids are, how educated, or how busy we are. Taking time for ourselves is not about money, social status, or race. It's not about earning it, or feeling guilty, or selfish, or like we don't need it. It's all about taking time to fully become alive and aware. It's alerting our life that we are now bringing the truth of who we are into play. We intend to no longer play small; instead, we step into our lives and our families in order to love, bless, and nurture.

This is both privilege and dilemma: to discover, honor, and practice the things that restore us. It is an issue of trust to believe that our choice will ultimately also restore them.

Because there are many dilemmas in the concept of self-care, we will acknowledge and address one at a time.

To be brave enough to tell our family we'd like to go to bed early, or that we want a night off (every week) to learn something new, or we want to make a dinner we love just because we love it, we are going to have to address the guilt of doing so.

Let's reframe selfishness; only then will you be ready to find concrete examples of what you most love. Because what our family needs is us, fully alive. What the world needs is us, fully alive.

And the only person preventing that from happening, is us.

Listening to Our Discontent

So we are brought back to discontent—something we need to pay more attention to. We don't listen to these inner rumblings; we listen for crisis. We can sniff out problems 10 days before anything happens, but discontent is more of an undercurrent for us. We don't want to say we're unhappy, or burned out. We can say we are stressed, but no one can really say why. Shouldn't we love the lives we worked very, very hard to create?

How dare we say it's not enough. Look—if I could only just get this closet decluttered...

And we go on.

But, we don't have sex with our husband or partner. We don't laugh with the kids. We don't bring ourselves fully to strategic volunteering—and often find excuses to not show up.

We. Don't. Want. Anything. But. To. Be. Left. Alone.

Oh, and we also want "Good Mom" status—if we can even define that.

There is a not-so-little study that never made it into the mom world—I suspect it's a conspiracy that it didn't. But I'm uncovering it, hoping for a gentle, subtle but sure upheaval of how we do life.

In his groundbreaking research, Marcus Buckingham, author of Your Strongest Life, uncovered something most of us already knew, but he brings it to us on a scale that reinforces it into our cells. In fact, just the scope and duration of his research are impressive enough, but it truly is his findings that change everything...

More than 1.3 million men and women were surveyed over 40 years, both here in the U.S. and in developed countries around the world. The findings: Greater educational, political, and employment opportunities have corresponded to more decreases in happiness for women, as compared to men. [1]

Read that again. More opportunity equals LESS HAPPINESS FOR WOMEN. They don't say why, but I believe it may come from all the time spent juggling family, kids, and work. It is a bit upheaving. It's a lot to keep up with and even the "good" isn't always good for us.

The second discovery in Buckingham's research: Though women begin their lives more fulfilled than men, as they age, they gradually become less happy. Men, in contrast, get happier as they get older.

Creeping unhappiness can seep into all aspects of a woman's life. When the researchers asked more specific questions, such as, "How satisfied are you with your marriage?" and "How satisfied are you with the things you own?" or "How satisfied are you with your finances?" the pattern was always the same: Women begin their life more satisfied than men, but wound up less satisfied in the end.

Key ages: Women's happiness with their marriage sinks below men's at age 39. Their satisfaction with their finances dips at age 41. By 44, they're more dissatisfied than men with the stuff they own.

Overall, the trajectory is consistent, and consistently downhill. By the time women reach age 47, they are, overall, less happy with their life than men, and the trend continues on down from there. However, for men, the trend goes upward—they get happier from the age of 39 on, in theory...

Of course, this doesn't mean that every individual woman becomes less happy or every man more happy—we've all got our own stuff going on. Nor does it mean that this darkening outlook on life is necessarily going to afflict you. You are a unique human being, blessed with the freedom to make your own choices, and so it's completely within your power to choose a life, and a perspective on life, that becomes more fulfilling as you get older.

However, right now, the two trends we see in the data are real and telling:

1. Over the last few decades, women, in comparison to men, have become less happy with their lives.
2. As women get older, they get sadder. [2]

No one will speculate what happens, why we end up unhappy and sad after years of giving so sacrificially. But I'm going to offer a thought that may resonate.

In her blockbuster book, Daring Greatly, Brene Brown talks about the voices inside our head, the voices that have everything to do with two core beliefs (I'll forego the lingo so we can really hear it):

- I did something bad/ not enough. (Code word: guilt)
- I am bad/ not enough/ too much. (Code word: shame) [3]

We don't deserve ... (time, money, care) ... because we are not enough.

As "typical" moms or moms with special needs

kids, or single moms, or with traveling husbands, or who aren't always home for a variety of reasons, moms with problems that can't always be solved, information that we don't always have, and resources we don't know exist — this message of shame and guilt hits us harder than most.

Those are the women who don't ask because someone is more deserving, or needy. Who believe they are not enough, so they play small —with self-care, with money, with life. Yet discontent remains. We cannot keep pretending we want one more scribble for the fridge, one more sports game to attend, one more dinner to make. We cannot pretend we're filled and happy when we live with the results of discontent: feeling empty, burned out, and/or resentful on some level.

So what can we do?

The answer lies in us. And I'm sure that makes you want to throttle me right now, but it's the quickest way to remedy our part of our family dysfunction. Because, if Mom is burned out, or feeling like her needs are unmet, there is a default to dysfunction.

What we are most afraid of is this: We'll take time out and others will think it selfish. We'll be judged. We'll come home and the house will be in shambles, the kids full on cereal, the clothes on the floors, and our mate will be complaining about how hard it was.

Here's the truth: Be the envy of all who find out. Deal with the mess. Listen to the mate. Give the kids veggies. Go to bed that night knowing and believing that it was a small price to pay for fresh perspective, soul breathing room, and more than an hour of uninterrupted time.

I've taken personal retreats, for an entire weekend, for 12 of the last 16 years. I have never been called selfish. I have considered myself spoiled on occasion, but not selfish. The worst thing that ever happened was my son's father required the same be given to him. Gladly I replied, "Just tell me when."

You know what happens when women find out I'm going away? They don't stop talking to me or think I'm a diva. They say, "I wish I was going with you."

And when I return, they always ask two things: How was it? And, what did you do? Truth is, you can't poach someone's restoration—you have to show up for your own.

What If I'm Selfish?

We have to overcome a few internal barriers when discussing self-care. We term it selfish but that's a catchall word for what we really experience.

There are three pieces to selfish. If we identify our own mix of the three, then we're halfway there: Guilt, Shame, and Fear.

One of my over 18,000 hours of therapy landed me with Dr. Bob Burbee at The National Institute of Marriage. I don't remember the context of the conversation, or the reason he said what he said, but I can guess I was complaining and/or whining to him. Dr. Bob slightly tilted his head, looked at me, and said, in the kindest, most compassionate voice I ever heard, "I wonder what would happen if you stopped abandoning yourself."

Me? I take breaks all the time. I do great things. In fact, I border on being selfish compared to every friend I have—how in the world was I abandoning myself?

I was doing so by not connecting with who I really was. By not advocating for a best-case-scenario-life, where my needs were included in the family structure.

By meeting everyone else's needs and acquiescing to a life that no longer fit me. But here's the worst part of it: I did it to myself. I couldn't blame my husband, my son, or any structure we had. I chose it.

When we abandon ourselves, and give to and live for others—out of fear, guilt, or shame—we abandon who we are and minimize our impact and place in the world. We do this to ourselves. No one does it to us.

Let me offer this, with immense compassion if you relate at all to this: Where are you abandoning yourself? Where are you disengaging to get it all done? Where does life feel 10 miles too wide and a tenth of an inch too shallow?

It's the easier path to not answer. But then, we

allow guilt, shame, and fear to rule. We listen to their voices: It doesn't really matter. I'm fine. I had a break last year, how many can I really ask for? They need xyz. I'm fine, really. I don't routinely pursue things that fill me. I don't create time to nurture myself. I don't address the callings I feel. I am perfectly fine to not rock the boat here and do whatever it takes to make this family well.

The culmination of fear, guilt, and shame that we wrap in the box of selfishness drives us to abandon ourselves, our needs, dreams, wants, and in many cases, passion, calling, and personhood.

OMG.

What's selfish is being the victim—we'll talk more about this later.

Holding others hostage with our anger, our feelings, and our demands for a perfect life ... yeah ... That's selfish.

Self-care is not optional. Self-care is a fiercely truthful way to show up in the world. Our highest goal cannot be to have a great dinner made. We cannot live under the disillusion that our actions FOR everyone trump our BEING. They never do.

Self-care stares in the face of guilt, fear, and shame. I matter. I want to stand here. I need to find myself so I can insert myself and stop blaming everyone else for abandoning myself.

Self-care is the foundation for our life. It's the foundation for our family because when we care for ourselves we show up—in authenticity, in love, in kindness, with a clearer path, direction, and connection to ourselves as well as everyone around us.

Manipulation

A truth I live, and my clients are introduced to early on, is this: When we do things for others to get something in return, we are manipulating. When we live out of guilt, shame, and fear, we manipulate others.

Manipulating is any form of: I do this so you do that. I take care of everyone so you should love me. I clean your laundry so you should listen to me. I take care of your needs so you should respect me. I burn myself out, don't find ways to take breaks, recharge or regroup because I care for you and this family. Now you all owe me. You owe me attention because I am a victim. You owe me a hug because I'm here. You owe me a relationship because I have so few friends any more.

All roots of manipulation begin when we avoid taking amazing care of ourselves.

Want the antidote?

It's a three-step process that really should be in a pill and sold all over the world for how profoundly it cures manipulation:

1. Believe you and your limits are worth listening to.
2. Identify what you need.
3. Make it happen in the most straightforward way possible.

If we get very clear on our needs, passions, and life, we stop projecting it onto everyone else. We begin to hold our life in our hands, looking at ourselves instead of looking away at others. When we begin to face our needs for sanity, value, and love, while figuring out how to address them, the enemies of guilt, shame, and fear start to limp away with no further foothold in our hearts.

15 Reasons Your Family Needs You Sane

1. Because they need a model so they can take care of themselves as adults without guilt.
2. Because our family doesn't always know what we need.
3. Because they can feel unsafe when we have unmet needs and are angry.
4. Because we can project our needs onto them and they don't actually need what we give them, but we can't see that.
5. Because we don't offer them our best.
6. Because we take them for granted.
7. Because we might no longer see the beauty in them.
8. Because we can begin to resent them.
9. Because we don't have fun with them anymore.
10. Because we "check out" with alcohol, reality TV, or spending or eating.
11. Because we don't really listen to them if we are spent.
12. Because we may not be patient with them.
13. Because we may become apathetic instead of intentionally connecting with them.

14. Because they need loving boundaries and consequences, and when we are out of sorts, we may not be able to offer clear headed parenting to them.
15. Because they deserve to see us at our best. It creates respect and a sense of identity for them.

Want Self-Care Options? Start Here

If something sparks your heart when considering self-care, then please, read no further. Whatever comes from inside, unsolicited, and bubbles up, is the truth. Go there.

However, if self-care has always been elusive and all you know is you actually don't like bubble baths, resent cleaning the tub before you get to bathe, and never have bath salts anyway, read on.

Maybe community classes sound good, or something that rekindles a love or art—classes, projects, museums. Maybe time alone at home or a coffee shop, curled up with a journal or a book. Friends can be an essential part of self-care also and the path back to sanity.

According to research studies, most moms want one of three things:

1. The day off parenting;
2. Sleep; or
3. Great food (that someone else cooked and cleaned up).

So start there. Choose one of those. Decide if you stay in or go out of the house. When the teeny tiny voice inside says it's probably better to stay in rather than wasting time going out, go out.

When the voices of the children need you as you leave, keep going. Trust that it's a process to find "Your Thing" that helps, nurtures, and gives to you.

Want some more clues?

What do you wish in the middle of the day? If only I could have five minutes to ... If only I pursued ... If I had $20, I'd...

These are your clues.

Very few moms get out of the gate and know

what they need. They just need practice getting out of the gate. But in time, the getting out gives way to: Where do I go? What would I love right now?

But here's the best way. Listen to yourself during times of stress or exhaustion. You don't even have to pull away to a quiet place, but right in the middle of it, ask yourself: What would I love right now? What do I need? Go there.

And this is where the magic happens... In the beginning, to hear where we want to go and what we want to do, we become connected to what matters to us, in the tiniest of choices. But it is in those tiny choices—when we address them and listen to them—that we start a new way of living.

How Self-Care Reveals Our True North

When my son was a few months old and I had some time to go somewhere by myself, all I knew was I wanted to go to a local bookstore and drink coffee. So I did. Decaf. With whip. And returned with pieces of my soul settled. Because I didn't just get coffee; I browsed. I wondered. I sat ... quietly. And pieces of who I was began to integrate with who I am now as a mom.

The next week, I brought a journal to the bookstore and took time to write incredibly basic and simple things—like what a 24-hour day was like for me, and what I missed most about not having a child, and a few dreams for my life.

A few weeks later, I browsed the magazines and my Teeny Tiny Voice told me to write an article.

A few weeks later, I brought a notepad and wrote ideas for an article.

Ultimately, I realized, I didn't have time for an article, but I did have time for a very small 50-word joke in Women's Day. That paid me $50.

And I wanted more. I started to save for a writer's conference. And over the next three years, I went to the conference, put a book proposal together, hired a coach, and was in hot pursuit of being published.

I ended up detouring and connecting with women over the radio on a morning show instead.

But it started with coffee.

Maybe you doubt the power of coffee and for the smallest of wishes think, Oh my gosh, I couldn't ask for THAT. I couldn't step into THAT. NOW??? It may seem like the thing you can't do, but it's the thing you must do.

The Teeny Tiny Voice telling you to wonder or wander, that's the exact thing that is needed. And let's be clear. It's not because everything gets revealed about your life over one bottomless cup of coffee. It's because you are standing up for your life and saying, "Here I am to meet you and I'm not willing to overlook you any longer. If all we can do today is one small coffee, then it's going to be the best coffee I've had all week. Whip, please!"

Now, the disclaimer here is this: The Teeny Tiny Voice is not saying to have an affair, to do drugs, to overeat, or get wasted in the local bar. The Teeny Tiny Voice is your ally to the highest possible good for, and in, you. It's not steering you to derail your life or the life of those you love. If this is the case and you cannot hear another voice, please, please, please find an AWESOME therapist and tell them you need to find your Teeny Tiny Voice again. They'll know what you're talking about.

The Whispered Truth

Not only do you matter, but you are irreplaceable.
You, with your beautiful life,
You, with your quirky bents,
You, with your imperfect parenting, and daily regrets for yelling,
Remain irreplaceable.

Besides...
The days you are bat sh*t crazy, you still deserve love.
The days you don't take a shower, you still deserve love.
The days you yelled, made a wrong call on their argument, punished unfairly, and erased the DVR by accident, you still deserve love.
If you deserve love, you deserve to treat yourself as one who does.
Do that.

I want to make such a strong case for self-care, that in the next generation, our children accept it as essential, not an option. We can live the example of taking responsibility for joyful, authentic lives.

Our daughters will bypass the curse of guilt and shame for stealing time away to regroup or take a nap. Our sons will help them make it happen. We can be part of a beautiful shift in modern motherhood.

:: DIY Mom Coaching:

1. What do I wish I could do when I'm in the middle of my day?
2. At night, what do I dream about before falling asleep?
3. When I talk to friends, what do I tell them I really want or need?

---

[1] Buckingham, Marcus. *Find Your Strongest Life*. Nashville: Thomas Nelson, 2009. p. 35.

[2] http://www.huffingtonpost.com/marcus-buckingham/whats-happening-to-womens_b_289511.html

[3] Brown, Brene. *Daring Greatly*. New York: Gotham Books, P.71.

CHAPTER 4
Practice #2: We Rediscover and Reinvent Ourselves

For you if you need to:

- Find yourself again
- Stop being resentful of taking your kids to their games/classes/schools
- Start your life anew in some way

I have heard, over and over through the tears of brave moms who dare to speak their truth: "I've lost myself and I don't know how to get myself back. There's no time. There's no money. Now what?"

Very often a mom will say this when her child(ren) are not yet school age. She's pulling her hair out staying home. Or she's working and there's nothing left for her at the end of a very long day—candles are burning at both ends. Often the family is frazzled, but she can no longer see this. She is holding it together, unsure how long it will last because she is coming undone.

I begin to explain to her how we cannot give what we don't have. She already knows this. She knows she is in trouble. Her body may be getting sick. She is not satisfied with life any more. This is nothing new. But, we both know she can live undone for a long, long time. She can harbor anger and resentment and still take the kids to school. She can live undone.

It's just that coming undone isn't really the problem. She knows, on a soul level, that this is not about performance, or not being efficient or forgetting to bring the cookies to school for the holiday gathering.

It's more dangerous than that.

When a mom comes to me and utters the words "I don't know who I am anymore," what I hear is this: I'm not giving my true self. I'm no longer showing up. I don't know what I'm supposed to offer beyond food, clothing, and shelter; and I know there's more.

When we lose ourselves—and it's understandable why we do—then we are missing so much of the reason we decided to have kids. I believe it's to share who we are, where we are, and pass on not only DNA, but also pieces of ourselves for the next generation.

We are to play fully in who we are, so they can see that, and learn that playing authentically is normal. Being who we are is giving them permission to be in the world. Living in our talents, abilities, gifts, and letting them see that this is where the magic happens—that's where we create a Life That's Enough.

Who Does That?

Many years ago, when I was speaking at a parenting conference, I met a woman who told me she was having difficulty connecting with her kids. She complained that they played too many video games and watched too much TV, and she wished she had something to get them moving.

During our conversation, I uncovered that she loved soccer and had actually played in college. I asked her if she still played. "No. I'm busy with my kids."

"Have you ever played soccer with them?"

"I hadn't thought about it before."

I'm thinking, I bet these kids don't even know their mom was on a college soccer team. In Spain...

Very often, the medicine for our family lies in who we truly are: Moms who want to matter—to ourselves and others—through our talents, abilities, and interests. Many times, these attributes that we so easily discard after having children, can not only shift our life, but can also help us to accomplish what we feel is missing in our families.

When we don't think about who we are, and what we have to offer, we leave off pieces of a puzzle that is our life. Those pieces fit answers to our current situation: How do I connect? Where do I volunteer? How do I matter?

Growing up, I took dance, music, and art lessons. Jordan's dad played football for four years in high school. My son wanted nothing to do with any of that. When Jordan was 10, in pursuit of my own dream, I learned how to surf. Within a year, Jordan wanted to try a surf camp and he DID! He returned for the next three years!

Three Ways to Rediscover Yourself

Discovering who you are (now, after having children) changes the family dynamic. By committing to sharing our passions and dreams with our kids, and believing in our choice to live authentically in the world, we will influence not only our children but also our family as a whole, by example.

It's the antidote to: I'm not enough/I'm too much. We can uncover all the beauty of who we are, and the sparkle we are in the world, and live it in front of our kids! We can offer the pathways and see if anything sparks something in them. Maybe our personal awakening will shed some light on something they are called to do.

Let's break down three areas of discovery: talents, abilities, and interests. If you're thinking, I have no idea, I don't even recognize myself any more, I ask you especially to accept the invitation to explore a little.

1. Talents

There are things we engage in that come easy to us. There's something in us that draws us to the activity and we lose all sense of time in doing this. There's often a natural interest, and when we try it, we find we pick up on it easily.

Interestingly enough, I've found that our talents often refresh us. They nurture a part of ourselves back to life. They reignite pieces of us that were sleeping. Very often, when we use our talents, we unexpectedly shift the world in some way. We bless others. We make an offering that someone else needed.

I know moms who are talented cooks, bakers, counselors, artists, musicians. They most often minimize their talent, taking for granted that they are in some way special. More often than not they act like, "Well, this is all I can do." And yet, it's the very thing that changes something in the air around them.

We know it for our kids, we forget it on our behalf...

I'm betting we each have a few talents, but it's life changing to find even one.

One of my talents? I can make little songs on a one-inch harmonica. No kidding. It makes me happy. It counts.

2. Abilities

When we've been trained to do something, it's considered an ability. Maybe we chose it in college. Or, we intended to be of service with it. It could be a thing we saw a need for in our family so we developed it. The abilities we have are a piece of self-efficacy. And self-efficacy means: "I can do this. It has meaning to me. I am able."

I have met many, many moms, and the ones who always humble me are the ones with the special needs kids. It never takes me long to realize their ability matches their challenge. They don't think so. They don't get it. But it's true every single time. I don't want to single anyone out, so I will only say this: When the children have more medical ailments than I can even understand, the moms' backgrounds—nursing. When homeschool is needed for intervention, the moms' backgrounds—teaching. When there are no great answers for their kids and they know they have to do something, they use their background—accounting, science, and management.

Whether you have a special needs child or not, what's your secret ability? What do you rock? Believe that the ability you have is the one your family most needs. Very often, it's what brought you alive in some way before you had children.

Reconsidering our abilities as a mom, reminds us of who we are and that we want to hold onto that part of ourselves.

3. Interests

You may be thinking: Are you kidding? If I had enough time for all this, I'd have already done it. I get that. But I also propose that the quality and quantity of what life currently consists of isn't fulfilling. We can change what we include in our life to make it more fulfilling—not only to us, but to our family as well.

Interests are rabbit trails and meandering daydreams, or questions about how the world works in some way. This is when we ignite our wonder, our "What if?" or our "I just want to."

At this point, you may be saying to yourself:

When the heck am I supposed to do this? Where's the money? Where's the time? All I want to do after dinner is crash. I understand that this can feel like adding one more thing to an already packed schedule. I get that, but what if we need to enlist help to make it happen?

What if we need to ask for a bit of time each week to go learn, or do, something that interests us? What if we put away the guilt, or stopped being afraid that the house will fall apart if we leave? What if?

The Lesson of the Trees

In 2008, a tree was discovered in remote Madagascar that rocked the scientific world. It was Xavier Metz, a cashew plantation owner, who came across a tree that grew to 66 feet and had 16 foot wide leaves. He immediately notified Kew Gardens in London. [1]

Dr. Dransfield, a world authority on palms, was called in to study the tree and to write an official report. He said that the leaves are the largest flowering plant in the world.[2] He cited it as a new species and marked it as the highlight of his career.

They called it Tahina Spectabilis, meaning "blessed or protected." (Tahina is the name of one of Metz' daughters.)

The tree looks like any other palm tree, except a large shoot grows from the top and marks the tree as vastly different from other palms. The shoot's branches burst into small white flowers that offer nectar to insects and birds. It is thought to be 30-50 years old.

But, there's something peculiar in its life cycle.

The flowering and blooming greatly dries up the resources of the plant. It gives all its nutrients, all its vital life force, to the flowers and it has nothing left for itself.

Within a few months after flowering, giving nutrients to the flowers and sustaining birds and insects, it collapses and dies.

I remember hearing that story on the radio when it first came out, instantly reminding me of moms. Many of us are 30-50 years old, giving everything we've got—literally sacrificing ourselves on some level for the good of our offspring, and community—and ultimately, we collapse.

There has to be another way. There has to be another angle, another way, beyond self-care, to not just honor our life but believe that it matters, believe that there is more to us than getting it all done. There has to be a way that doesn't lead to our self-destruction.

Let me tell you about another tree that may hold answers for us. A way that reveals thriving.

Sam Van Aken, a Syracuse University art professor and award winning contemporary artist, grew up on his family's farm in the northeast. Van Aken says that he finds his inspiration in "nature and our relationship to nature." In 2008, he combined his two interests in an exhibit called "Eden," where he grafted vegetables together to make odd plants that also doubled as art. From there, he had the idea to graft parts of trees together.

The artist takes a base fruit tree and makes slices in the tree. He then takes branches from other fruit trees and tapes them together—sliced edges facing each other. In time, the branches fuse into the trunk, and within a year or two, there are different fruits from the same tree. I've included a link to Sam's TED talk [3] so you can actually see the tree. It's a little mind bending to see almonds, peaches, apricots, and plums grow on the same tree.

He considers this "sculpture through grafting." He creates the branches through the timing of blooms, and the fruit it produces. He wants to communicate, through this medium of art, a shift in the way we perceive life in general. [4]

The art of thriving. Having a base stem and adding pieces that look different but still bloom without destroying the base, is a multifaceted approach to life as a mom, that is so revolutionary, we may not even understand how profoundly beautiful it is.

The graftings are NOT our kids, our spouse/partner, our job, or our duties.

We may feel that way because there are so many pieces of life that feel grafted onto us. We love it all, it becomes part of us, so it seems like everything outside of our body is grafted onto us.

But this example holds a beautiful lesson of the deeper work of thriving.

The graftings are our Talents, Abilities, and Interests. The things that make us unique and beautiful. They not only sustain us, but also give life to others without destroying the base, which is us. These are the grafted pieces that breathe life into us—that provide us with a place to bloom so we're not one dimensional.

The pieces we graft onto us may not look like much at first, but they bloom into a gorgeous life that is built on giving, and not just martyring ourselves. We may come to discover that these pieces were a part of us all along.

We find a photography class and feel like it is "home" to us. We learn a software program and we feel alive. I believe it's because the pieces that seemed so foreign to us, drew life from us to meet them—like those pieces were surging in us all along, and they just needed a place to release it all.

Sometimes, when we go out of our comfort zone to find things that matter greatly to us, we find ourselves and our very lives. We become more than one dimensional. We start to be interesting and see the world differently. Life begins to feel like it is opening up, because we are opening up.

Although there is some sacrifice the family makes for us to achieve this, in the end they will feel they are recompensed with a mom who is alive. The gifts, talents, and abilities used are considered pieces of self-efficacy.

Self-efficacy is best described as what I believe I can do with my skills under certain conditions that I choose. I believe I am capable because I am able to do things over time and this experience proves to me I am able. [5]

Unlike any other role in life, as moms we have very little choice. Lunches have to be made. Life has to happen. We go to work, feed the kids, make lunches for the next day, take a shower, and repeat on a mind-numbing daily basis. This is not self- efficacy. There is no challenge, no shift or change, no life.

The studies on self-efficacy all conclude the same: With it, we thrive. Without it, we are, at best, bored, and at worst, depressed and stressed. This holds true for adolescents, adult career men and women, and women who are moms.

So to really thrive as a mom, we have to a have a life that includes attempting and experiencing over a period of time something that we can tackle that proves to ourselves we are capable and, quite honestly, freaking brilliant. The cornerstone piece to all of this is that we do something we don't normally do during the day, something we feel would be amazing. This is where gifts, talents, and abilities come in.

When we follow what we already have interest in, or love, and carve time and money to learn it, we are 10 steps toward self-efficacy. We find we are engaging in the world in a different way. We are finding ourselves and also using resources from our very being that would otherwise lie dormant.

Dormant.

The only tree that goes dormant is the one that blooms after 50 years and then dies. The other tree, with a variety of life glued on it, stuck to it, nourishing the other pieces that are on it—it thrives.

I want to say this: Self-efficacy is the foundation of sanity. It tells us we are alive. We matter. We are vital. We can engage in our lives beyond care-taking and meeting needs. We are an individual and bring life to the world as the world gives us life.

It's difficult to say that we don't need self-efficacy or that we don't have time for it, but rediscovering you—giving to your family, finding yourself in talents and gifts, using them, watching the world change shape because of it —are all pieces of you that, in turn, will make you a different mom.

How?

When a mom feels full and alive, living from a place of strength, she realizes she wants her kids to feel this way too. She begins to look for ways that the kids can feel like they can accomplish things. She loosens the grip on control. She cheers them on.

A mom who understands self-efficacy will no longer push care-taking into control. She has no need to micromanage everyone and everything because she needs time to put into her other pursuits.

The truth is, when a mom shifts in herself, she changes as a parent as well. With a little awareness, she realizes what needs to happen and that she can alter the way she sets up the family, creating different opportunities for everyone to find self-efficacy—for everyone to bloom.

As an aside, research shows that women who feel confident as moms, and report high self-efficacy in parenting, have children who have low anxiety and are less victimized by their peers. [6]

Let me make this clear: No mother has ever failed her kids because she carved some time to rediscover herself. In fact, the failures, bitterness, and parental breakdowns occur when we abandon ourselves, default to living in response to everyone else and fail to factor in ourselves, operate out of defaulting and not out of a self.

This is about reframing who we are and what

our lives have to offer our families. Becoming responsible for and infusing our lives with talents, gifts, and abilities makes us phenomenal.

Where that takes our family is up for discussion in our next chapter. Because when we start dreaming about the potential of our life, we can't help but imagine the potential of our family unit.

:: DIY Coaching Questions:

1. What fun did you engage in pre-motherhood?
2. What ability might you have that can be seen as a gift to your family?
3. What's one dream that you always wanted to pursue?

---

[1] http://www.dailymail.co.uk/news/article-508861/Discovered-The-self-destructing-palm-tree-flowers-100-years.html

[2] http://www.dailymail.co.uk/news/article-508861/Discovered-The-self-destructing-palm-tree-flowers-100-years.html#ixzz3CAc8w33L

[3] http://new.livestream.com/tedx/manhattan2014/videos/43864399

[4] http://www.epicurious.com/articlesguides/chefsexperts/

interviews/sam-van-aken-interview

[5] **Maddux, James, E.** Self – Efficacy: The Power of Believing You Can. George Mason University (in press). Snyder, C. R., & Lopez, S. J. (Eds). Handbook of positive psychology. New York: Oxford University Press p. 5-6

[6] http://www.academia.edu/2329045/Analysing_Mothers_Self-efficacy_Perception_towards_Parenting_in_Relation_to_Peer_Relationships_of_5-6_year-old_Preschool_Children

CHAPTER 5
Practice #3: We Create A Vision, Not Live Overwhelmed

For you if you need:

- A sieve to run things through to say *yes*
- A reason to say *no* besides "I don't want to"
- Something to live and parent toward

When we realize we have everything it takes to both unfold and create our family, it's helpful to look outside the box of parenting books to piece together what makes sense. We need concepts that speak to, move, drive, and motivate us as leaders of our families. Since becoming an effective leader is so important, we'll borrow the next practice from the business world: Vision.

No company on the planet survives without a vision/mission statement. This gives them a belief, or a direction, or a reason for being. Designed and crafted with intention, this statement is shared with all employees and creates a culture that sustains their presence in the world.

Here are a few famous companies' vision statements:

Amazon: "Our vision is to be earth's most customer centric company; to build a place where people can come to find and discover anything they might want to buy online."

Apple: "Apple is committed to bringing the best personal computing experience to students, educators, creative professionals and consumers around the world through its innovative hardware, software and Internet offerings." [1]

The term vision is tossed around a lot when a company is starting up, or in a boardroom when focus is needed, or at times when business professionals want to give direction and meaning to their company. This is because vision isn't a fluff word or concept; it's hardcore —it helps them make decisions, it helps them to say no, to decide who to hire and who to fire, to decide where their expenses go, what products to sell and how, what to invest in, and ultimately, their success or failure.

Sounds like a secret sauce for raising a family, doesn't it?

The problem is, it's not a concept heard on playgrounds. It isn't on the radar for moms. We don't have money to hire a business coach to craft the exact correct vision that will make our family work. And, we don't think in terms of moving toward the future because we are too busy responding to so many things in the present.

I get it.

BUT, when we have a vision, everything changes. We get very clear on what kind of help we need in parenting, what and why we say yes or no. What matters to us.

I bumped into the vision concept in Stephen Covey's *7 Habits of Highly Effective People.*

Two months after my son was born, I understood, all too well, sleep deprivation, schedules, and laundry. I was somewhere between being bored out of my mind, asking myself if this was all there is of my life now, and wanting to be the best wife and mom on the face of the planet. It was then that I found Covey's book.

I cannot recommend this as an early parenting book, but for me, it made it very clear that I needed to delegate (to whom?), to parse out the important from the urgent (it was all urgent), and to prioritize self-care (which was a golden nugget). Although much of the book described the business world, I gleaned something I already suspected that might be GREAT for parenting: "Begin with the end in mind," i.e., vision. Since brain cells were not immediately replaced from childbirth, and postpartum depression was in full throttle, I focused on self-care in the beginning, and only later, worked on a vision.

What A Vision Is

One of the best descriptions of a vision comes from Cameron Herold, a Canadian CEO living in Phoenix, and the former chief operating officer of 1-800-GOT-JUNK. I figure a successful business that removes what we declutter is worth listening to.

Cameron takes a cue from athletes. *"I saw how the best jumpers used visualization techniques. They'd stand on the runway and use their hands to block out the view of anything but the high jump bar and the landing pit. They'd look at the bar, visualize their run up, takeoff, step, and roll over the bar. They could see it all, as if a movie were playing in their head. Why shouldn't entrepreneurs and executives do the same thing?"*

Herold used what he calls "vivid visions" to increase sales from $2 million to $125 million. Today Herold is a speaker and coaches CEOs. *"A vivid vision starts when an entrepreneur, founder, or CEO plants one foot in the present and then leans out and places the other in the future, the what could be."* [2]

A vision takes companies from $2 million to $125 million. It guides investments of time, energy, and money. As moms, we're the CEOs of our family. If we're married, our husbands most likely aren't even thinking in these terms, but when we explain it, many are on board. If we're alone, a vision is all the more critical.

A vision statement will hold us when the seams

are falling apart. While it's not written in stone, it's a rock to land on most days. We can change and alter it when it doesn't fit or we wanted something in error, but for the most part, it helps us steer in the directions most in our heart, teaches us where we lack, and reminds us why we are trying to get where we're going.

I hired a coach to help me get a handle on my life and a book I was writing at the time. Jordan was settled into Pre-K (and just a few months before OCD and Tourette's would become household guests), so some time opened up for me to work on it. My coach and I anchored the project in a vision for the work and me. In fact, some of the wording included "advocating for women," "helping women connect with each other," etc.

As I was writing, really using the vision to ground and encourage my work, it was at that time that I wondered why we don't, as moms, cast a vision far and wide for ourselves and our families.

So I decided to craft a small vision on Jordan's behalf, even though he was so young. I wrote out what mattered, getting input from his dad to add anything I left out. We decided what was important to us and came up with: athletics, another language, creativity, music, social skills, free time, and academics. I wanted him to be able to travel to another country, and to learn how to deal well with money.

Over the years, through all our ups and downs, I looked again and again at the vision crafted on his behalf. I often wondered if he would ever do, or be able to do, the things I wrote. But regardless, I engaged the vision.

By following and utilizing my small vision statement, I was able to do many things to help Jordan, and myself, achieve our vision.

I found a satellite community that took on art, music, and language for homeschoolers. Although funds were tight, every week we went to a local coffee shop run by a man from Japan that had Asian ice cream, cookies, soda, and bread. It was our favorite day of the week. We played chess because that was the only board game they had there. He beat me most days. We had time for reading and writing and math, while still allowing him time to play outside and with friends from the neighborhood.

This concept not only changes motherhood, it brings it back to what it was supposed to be—a visionary woman raising her family to be visionary men and women in the world. That doesn't mean famous, or rich. It means purposeful, intentional, grateful. More profoundly, is the impact vision has on kids.

10 Potential Shifts That Happens To Kids With A Family Vision

1. They understand the rules—because the rules make sense in a larger context of where we're all heading.
2. They understand "who we are" as a family —because there is an identity now.
3. They have a context for understanding decisions—because it makes sense for what we're moving toward.
4. They have language to discuss things— their questions will be in regard to the communicated direction.
5. They feel safe because they know what to expect.
6. They have a foundation of living toward a vision that they can choose or reject as they make their own way in the world.
7. They can find friends who reflect the

family values, direction, and culture.
8. Anxieties can decrease because there is less force and hurry used for a disconnected life.
9. They understand where they fit in the larger vision and how they are not just considered but an integral part of it.
10. They know they can trust us to make good decisions toward everyone's best interest.

A vision is something bigger than us, something that's not yet but still lives in a hope or deep belief. Sometimes we wonder if we should try, dream, go toward ... And, the answer is, Yes, try that. Holy yes. Go with it and see what happens!

Where there is no vision, the people are unrestrained. Proverbs 29:18

When we don't create a vision for ourselves, we say yes to anything. When we don't create a vision for our children, we allow them to do whatever. When we don't create a vision for our family unit, we spend time, money, and energy and still we are not happy.

But, a mom with a vision is a world changer, a game changer, a visionary. She completely upheaves the status quo of the culture in her home. She carves, completes, and has reasons why she did something, instead of excuses why she didn't.

Wanting Change, Not Wanting to Change

Change is scary and brings up resistance we didn't even know we had. I know this firsthand. Moms come to me for coaching, wanting something (anything) to change—them, their home, their kids, their relationship. They are open, willing, and brutally honest. They face the intake form. They pay up front. They want change. I know it's not just any change though. It's targeted, authentic, life transforming change, specifically tied to their own skills, life, and home. They want a phenomenal family life and to be a phenomenal mom.

So we begin. They are unafraid. Ready to take on my challenges. Ready—until we get to week two or three.

It is somewhere between week two or three that we set up a path—a loose direction, generated by Mom, with all options on the table for what life could look like. Then, I issue the challenge: Make a personal and/or family vision.

They will do both. They have ideas. This is going to be good.

And then we get to the next session. It was a tough week: hubby was traveling, the kids were awful, work was more than expected, the dog needed the vet, there was no more toilet paper in the house so she needed an emergency run to the store... One excuse after another.

There is no vision statement.

I used to spend a session talking through the resistance, working through the fear in the most non-therapy type ways I could. I used to give another shot, try another week, provide 1000 alternate ways of coming up with a vision.

It wasn't done again.

More excuses: The in-laws came over. She decided to start a business. She wants a different job. There needs to be more money, and after the kids get out of kindergarten, once summer is here ... and on and on. No vision. In fact, it's a great session of light bulb moments when they realize that without a vision, they will constantly be making these fly by the night decisions that plunge the family further into overwhelm, chaos, and lack of direction (not to mention connection).

This is personal growth, and it takes time, and challenge, and attention. Most moms never ask themselves WHY they do or don't do things. They just accept that the closets—and life—are cluttered. I'll clean them later. We rarely take time to ask why the closets are cluttered, instead finding it easier to blame everyone else for throwing coats on the ground.

So, by the next session there is a start toward a few wants. Lots of fears. I don't push through fears. They protect us. They teach us. If we'll listen, they have nuggets to share with us.

8 Common Mom Fears About Change

1. Failure: I messed it all up, I WILL mess it all up, I've messed it up this far, maybe I'll just keep going. We figure if we leave it alone, we may be miserable, but at least it's running. Life, family, marriage, our relationship with our tweens, it's what we know. We don't trust ourselves to make a better choice, to turn the tables, to change life or even tweak it.

2. Guilt: I should have, Why didn't I...Guilt often starts before we even do anything. This leaves no room for even considering change because the What ifs are so tough, we stop short. If we do make a change, often it won't be "good enough" so we lose either way.

3. Success: What if I pull this off? Then what? We may have to make other changes or concessions in our lives if we're successful. Many times, I didn't think I could actually do something, and when it happened, I had to make other sacrifices. This fear is the fear of further loss or change that we didn't bargain for.

4. Unknown: I don't know enough. We don't know what we don't know, and for many of us, that's enough to keep status quo right there. No questions asked. We're done before we start.

5. Shame/ Perfection: I'm not enough. Often, the standard is perfection. If we're not perfect (or our home, kids, marriage aren't), then we're less than. We all know intuitively that no decision is perfect, which unnerves us before we start.

6. Others' Reaction: What if they don't like it or handle it well? Then what? We are very aware that we deeply affect others. We shift and the whole family shifts with us. Which leads to: Let's not rock the boat.

7. Doing It Wrong: What if we don't nail it the first time? What if we want change and we go about it all wrong? When we don't have room for error, this one shuts us down before we even get started.

8. Missing Something: Savvy moms know if we make a change and head in a direction, we will, by default, be leaving out other things. What if we need those other things and don't realize it? What if we completely miss out on something the kids needed? Then what?

It's not enough to simply plow through these fears. They are real. Whether we have one fear, or a combination, these can shut down our vision for our family; they can stop us from succeeding in life or making any changes that we hold close and wish for.

When we're stopped for too long, we get

resentful. We start blaming. We're off the track we know we could be on. And then we need a little nudge, inspiration, or support.

But, ultimately, to change, we have to face the fears.

Secrets To Change: The Shallows

So what do we do once we see fears?

We get off the 100-foot diving board and go to the 3-foot shallow end. We start small, take baby steps toward change. Staying alert to messages trying to inform or protect us, we can take one safe step at a time, addressing little voices instead of plowing through them.

As we consistently wade forward toward creating a vision, one of the eight fears above will inevitably kick in. If it's addressed, respected, and listened to, we'll learn what needs attention. This helps us move forward with confidence because we aren't in the deep end, plunging our family, like a cannonball, and ourselves off on huge shifts of change.

We are wading slowly and carefully toward a life we love, and doing it at a pace everyone is okay to tread with us at.

We don't change entire weekends to match our vision. We just ask for a few hours on Saturday. Family may resist, because you know, change is scary.

But, once we face and overcome our own fears, compassion for their fears and resistance to change comes more easily—because we faced what they are facing.

A mom with a vision believes in things bigger than her fear—love, faith, legacy, and family. She dares to dream, to put one foot forward into the future. This is truly a phenomenal mom. Not that she forces it all to happen, but that she listens for the little spark of the dream in her heart.

So, if you're ready for an official challenge, try a few DIY questions. Dream a little. Imagine what's possible. Face a few fears and try it in increments. (Yes, actually, you were made for this, you gifted, sane, wise mom you.)

:: DIY Coaching Questions:

1. What's your dream for your family five years from now?
2. Who is five years ahead of you in parenting and family life? What do you love about their life?
3. Which fear might stop you from moving toward a vision for your family?

---

[1] http://www.scribd.com/doc/26265827/Mission-Vission-statements-of-Companies#scribd
[2] http://www.forbes.com/sites/richkarlgaard/2015/01/05/vivid-vision-for-success/

CHAPTER 6
Practice #4: We Live In Our Power, Not Our Anger

For you if you need to:

- Understand and work on anger
- Change relationships to, and perspective on your kids
- Stop driving yourself crazy
- Quickly shift parenting styles because a current interaction is not working

According to my social media stats, moms have a very undercover, but very powerful, anger issue. When I tweet or post on anger, nearly no one hits "like" or shares, or passes it along. Ever. But when I send a private e-zine to their inbox, over 60% of everyone opens it. Normally, it's around 20%.

I get it. There is a mom code that we often abide by. You already know it.

This code states that we look like we know what

we're doing, we rarely ask for help, and we never admit to being angry. There's very few ways to get out of this cycle. Most of us have very few women we can trust and reach out to, and nearly no one, other than a therapist, whom we can go to and say, "I have an anger issue and I need to get over it."

We know we cannot be the only one, but we don't know how to constructively talk about it without fear of someone calling social services on us. Quite frankly, this isolation feeds the anger.

So, in the face of this isolation and shame (and because I have several witnesses who would out me in a skinny minute), I raise my hand and introduce myself to the group... Hi. My name is Vikki, and I'm a recovering angry mom.

(I'll imagine the response of a few thousand moms: *Hi Vikki ;-)*)

We're in good company.

Let's start with a base line understanding. The physical reasons our kids get angry apply to us as well: tiredness, hunger, pain, or overload from the day. Before we get any further, let's just pinky promise each other to always check these physical reasons first before we get into the deeper reasons behind anger. There's no use in digging deep when really all we needed was a 20-minute power nap and a little chocolate.

But sometimes, that's not it. We can't place it and need a little help. Here are a few other reasons to consider:

14 REAL Reasons You May Be ~~Pissed Off~~ Angry

1. You're hurt (emotionally).
2. You're afraid.
3. You didn't address something.
4. Something triggered a childhood response.
5. You're frustrated.
6. Something was unresolved and came back around.
7. You were ignored (again).
8. You don't feel respected.
9. You don't feel valued.
10. You feel ashamed.
11. You feel guilty.
12. You feel powerless.
13. You feel alone.

14. You feel misunderstood.

This chapter addresses the consistent anger, even a low current running under our skin. Somewhere there's a source. If it's not a physical source, it's an emotional source.

It's Not About The Jacket

Let's look at a scenario: You walk in from a long work day. There is a jacket on the floor. Again. Clutter drives you crazy. You don't feel respected. You yell. You give consequences.

In fact, though, you realize it's not just the jacket. You yell about dirty dishes and messy rooms. Anger has a way of feeding itself and looking for reasons to stay alive. Pretty soon, you're getting blank stares and fearful faces, and kids racing to pick up the jacket out of fear. At some point, you hate yourself. It was like an anger binge and now you're seeing the effects. It's miserable.

You're making dessert for dinner to apologize. You are sorry. You're not sorry. You don't know what else to do.

It all started with a jacket...

Let's own the message and power of anger. It is sending us a message, letting us know that something is triggering us in some way. We need to be listening.

How could a jacket trigger me?

It could feel like we are being disrespected. Or maybe that we're being ignored, or didn't train them well, and they are going to be in prison with a felony because we stink as a mom ... could be all of it together.

Whatever it is for you, tune into it, because to the rest of the house, it's just a jacket.

The jacket is on the floor. The voices begin: They never listen to me. How many times do I have to tell them so they'll listen? What am I not getting across??? They disrespected me again. And I'm not going to take it any more. It's been a tough day. You would think they could do this one small thing. You would think they could even try. I'm not going to say anything ... (enter silent and seething status).

Introducing the voice of the mom ego...

When we move from an objective, "the jacket is on the floor," to anything emotional, believing this is about us—we're making it personal. The jacket is on the floor because they are disrespecting me, they never listen to me, they don't care about me. All mom ego.

Our mom ego positions us to be right, to be listened to, to get our way—now. If our ego doesn't get its way, it gets louder. And more forceful. And has no other tricks up its sleeve other than to repeat itself, demand, yell, and pull a tantrum. Sounds like the kids, doesn't it? ;-)

So, if we can spot the mom ego and the demanding "it's all about me" aspect, then all that's left is the jacket—and we can learn to address that.

Lucky for you, I have over 18,000 hours of counseling and have been working on this FOREVER and would love to reveal one of many shortcuts. It's ridiculously powerful and simple, and it's going to make sense, but it's not easy. In fact, although I'm offering one phenomenal answer to anger in the next few pages, I assure you of days and weeks and months ahead, of striving to apply it.

As I stated in the beginning, I'm in successful recovery, which means there are rare but brightly shining moments where I realize, mid-stream, that I'm angry. I pull out this exact shortcut below. Every time.

It's All About Me

So, the best thing to do is remove ourselves from any situation and come back to it when we cool down. Absolutely nothing will make the momma ego happy—except yelling louder. There are five keys to calming down.

Let's look at each one.

When we're away from whatever bee is in our bonnet, we have the chance to face ourselves and listen.

1. First, we have to figure out what exactly we're feeling and let that be known. Does the jacket bring out fear, guilt, disrespect, powerlessness, feeling not heard, or a combination? Exactly what is the emotional cocktail we're shaking? Check the list above; this is key one.

2. Secondly, armed with an emotion, we can ask, What do I need to make this better? What do I need when I feel guilty, or what do I most want when I feel disrespected? This is a second key.

3. The third key takes fierce courage to ask ourselves, What is the earliest memory I have where I felt like this? Identifying this may unlock childhood stuff, but if it's not addressed, that childhood of ours comes out to play in our current family life and it's not only confusing but devastating.

If this step is too difficult, or if you find the same memory or answer over and over, get to a therapist who can unlock it. Otherwise, our kids will always be wondering what just happened and we're the only ones who really know.

4. Fourthly, we find another key when we ask, "What do I most need right now?" The shortcut answer is always self-compassion. We cannot give what we don't have. If we give this one to ourselves and not demand our family members give it to us after we've just yelled about a jacket, we're nearly transformed. But we may need other things as well—respect, attention, or time. Whatever it is, this is the step where we offer it to ourselves.

5. The final key: What do I most desire to happen when I go back out (as objectively as possible)? This may take a few tangled minutes, but there will be a final answer. Do I need the jacket picked up? Yes, and all the clutter decluttered. Have I put in place expectations and consequences for this? Um... no. Okay. So, we go back out there, apologize like a mother, and clearly state the new expectations about jackets and clutter in general, as well as natural consequences. No sarcasm. No anger. Just pure parenting.

It may look like this:

I feel disrespected.
I'm feeling this way in all areas of my life right now.
I've felt this way since I was in High School. Wait, since I was in Jr. High.
Nobody listened to me.
I'm going to listen to and respect myself. I respect me.
I'm going to go back out and, after apologizing, explain respect.

This is really not about the jacket.

Or:

I feel nobody listened to me.
I've felt this way since I was little.
I'm going to commit to listening to myself for
even just three minutes every single day.
I can go back out there, with apologies, and
explain that when I ask for something to be done,
to have iPhones put down, have eye contact, and
some sort of verbal response, any action that I'm
asking for, so I know they are listening.
This kind of is about the jacket.

Or:

Nobody listened to me.
This makes me furious.
I've been furious all day and was furious before I
got home.
I need to go work out after work.
I will go back out, apologize hard, and just go
work out.
It's not about the jacket.

Disclaimer: this is the stuff of my 18,000 hours of therapy. Your solution may be very different from this situation. I'm not intending to give professional advice or solutions, please seek out any professional help you need.

Finally, if we really do the work, consistently (or just more often than not), then one day, out of the blue, we will absolutely get to watch this same scenario unfold completely differently.

Hi kids! So great to see you! Whose jacket is on the floor? Please pick it up—or in a few days I'll be putting it in my closet.

There are other options. Anger is telling us something.

Sometimes it's actually easier to think everything is about us all the time. It gives us an illusion of control, of blame, almost bordering on being a victim. Depending on our upbringing, and what feels "normal," saying, "It's all on me," keeps us in the game when really we should be on the sidelines.

The Sidelines: It's Not About Me

Blissfully, there is a counterpoint to "It's about me," the other end of the spectrum: "It's not about me." Everything isn't personal.

In fact, much of the time, it isn't about us at all. When we get better at realizing what needs to be cleaned up in our own emotional kitchen, and what doesn't belong there, the mom ego takes her toys and goes to play somewhere else. She has no welcome if it's not about her. We get to watch from the emotional sidelines. How does this look? I think you're going to love it.

Let's take the same jacket scenario and run it through the ridiculously powerful phrase, "This is not about me."

There is a jacket on the floor. Again. Clutter drives you crazy. You don't feel respected. You DON'T yell. You give consequences. In fact, it's not just the jacket, but you'll deal with the rest of the house another time. For now, it's time to deal with the jacket on the floor.

"Carly? I'm home!"

"Yeah, Mom?" Muffled from the bathroom where

she's taking selfies. Again.

"The jacket is on the floor, again. Please come pick it up."

Or: *"The jacket is on the floor, so I'm going to take it until Friday like we discussed."*

Or: *"The jacket is on the floor, again. I'll expect your whole room to be clean before dinner at 6:30, like we discussed. I'll get the jacket for you this time."*

Pretty soon, you're at dinner, realizing the jacket is in its place, her room is clean, and the family can happily chat about the day.

Is this really possible? Does it really happen? All. The. Time. When a mom quickly realizes a situation is not personal, is not a direct hit to her, and just needs an objective response.

By being on the sidelines, we allow our children to take responsibility for their actions. We are allowing a situation to be all about them. It's truly a phenomenal mom who allows kids to feel the weight of their actions WITHOUT all the drama, yelling, shame, and guilt.

When children, tweens, and teens understand their responsibility for their actions, choices, and, ultimately, their life, we put them in the power position for their own life. And we stay in our emotional kitchen, happily buffing the counters, singing Bruno Mars, "You're amazing ... Just the waaaay you arrrrre," and forgetting if you're singing about yourself or the family.

But My Kid Still Doesn't Pick Up The F!*& Jacket

There will be times when there is a check mark on everything suggested above. Expectations clearly communicated. Consequences delivered. And the jacket is still on the floor. They just resist.

Other than a true professional diagnosis of oppositional defiance, resistance can come in many forms, including ignoring a routine, choosing questionable clothes or friends, fighting bedtime, or walking on jackets on the floor.

Now we're angry. We want to yell, demand, shame, and guilt them into dealing with the situation. We can pull our authority and keep the power play going, or we can shift gears into understanding. Maybe there's an opportunity to understand them here ... maybe they are making sense about something ... I wonder what's really going on—maybe it's not about the jacket for them. If we stay in an openhearted place, maybe we can seek to understand their truth—whatever it is.

Here are a few AWESOME questions to ask in a situation where nothing is making sense and you want to understand:

- What do you think about this situation?
- What don't you like about it?
- What makes you sad, angry, etc. about this?
- What do you think I'm asking of you?
- What do you want to do instead?

We may find out that really, they want attention and this is how they're getting it. They may need fun. Or feel lonely, sad, afraid, or confused. Or they may want to share something with us, or to matter. 90% of the time, the situation we are trying to figure out is about a deeper issue.

Whatever truths you uncover will be the golden

center of connection. It will help you understand them in a completely different way and realize that anger is always a distant second to understanding.

If we can stop hiding and stop being afraid of it, we may find anger is fire and power, and truth and life, all rolled up in our soul, pouring out from our mouth. The secret is to hold it, look at it, take deep breaths, and don't lose eye contact with it. We need to seek and ask it what it has to tell us, because it is telling us something.

It may tell us our mom ego is lying to us again. Or that we need to let our child(ren) face consequences for their choices. Or that switching the self-talk may serve us better to understand, connect, and love.

If we'll listen openheartedly, we may be able to find compassion and our voice all rolled together to help us make incredible shifts in our life. When we move forward in processing anger with our kids, I nearly promise on my dog's favorite biscuit that you will find every other relationship, where anger is destroying things, start to heal. Not even kidding. Whatever true and good work we do is collateral blessing in our life.

Also, I nearly swear that when we're ready to be a safe and healing place, another mom may pop into our lives and confide, "I think I have an anger issue." And you'll realize that your recovery means there's hope for her. This is the practice of a phenomenal mom: understanding our ego and anger and believing our children are more important than any of that. Knowing that as we practice changing our responses, we allow our families the gift of not living in fear for our next "moment." We commit to being phenomenal each time.

Once we have a handle on understanding anger, we realize how much connection we've been missing. We'll do anything to make up for lost time. Read on.

:: DIY Coaching Questions:

1. Next time there is a "jacket on the floor" of life, say to yourself: "This is about me," and run through the 5 Keys to listen for what's really going on emotionally.
2. Next time there's a conflict, say, "This is not about me" and allow the child to face their choices or actions.
3. Make a list of at least three insecurities you deal with in yourself. Watch how one of those plays out in conflict with others.

CHAPTER 7

Practice #5: We Commit To Unwavering Connection

For you if you need to:

- Deepen the connection with your kid(s) but don't know how
- Understand how to build a bridge when the connection is broken
- Find new ideas for recharging family unity

It seems to me that we always have an agenda. Almost always. We teach, train, correct, give consequences, feed, lecture, fix, remind, and tuck in. But, when do we just enjoy our kids? When do we let them be, and engage with them —without trying to change them in some way?

Really being present with a child/tween/teen, without judgment, takes humility. It teaches us that they are amazing just as they are. They know things. They can teach us things. They are beautiful and quirky and unique. They deserve to be seen. It affirms them and validates their existence in the world.

A single mom once came to me because she was working, and going to school, and had a three year old. She didn't even know where to begin to interact with him; he bothered her during her homework and she ended up reprimanding him most of the evening they were together. She wanted to watch basketball but couldn't because he demanded attention. He hit other kids in school.

I asked her, "When DID he earn attention, presence, adoration?" I knew she was busy, probably with more on her plate than she was even telling me. But, I also knew her little boy needed her in ways that he could not express, except in acting out. At least then he got attention ... but the worst kind. So, I asked her to intervene. I told her to really look him in the eye, to really see him and have fun with him. THEN make time for schoolwork.

This takes time, of course. For them, there were weeks it looked like nothing was changing. Eventually, though, she settled into a routine. One that not only included him but welcomed him. She learned what triggered him, and ultimately, made an appointment with a specialist that changed the course of both their lives.

Connection Matters More Than We Ever Know

In an article from the University of Berkeley, there is a profound research study that questions if addiction is actually as chemically driven as once thought, or if there are other factors involved.

Bruce Alexander, a psychologist and researcher from Vancouver, uses mice that are in an isolated cage. They are offered cocaine in their water, and they become so addicted to it, they ultimately die. But Alexander wondered if he changed the cage, added a little "town" with things to do and more mice, and he kept the cocaine as an offering, would the mice still go for it? If he offered two bottles—one with the drug and one without, which would the mice ultimately go for?

The mice in Rat Town almost never went back to the cocaine water. They chose the other water. They were happy and connected. They rejected the drug.

The researchers pushed the envelope a little further. They let the rats get hooked on cocaine for 57 days. Then removed them to Rat Town. Guess what happened? They stopped taking the drug.

This cutting edge research date? 1970.

So, with this timeframe in mind, there was a human side to this that was very similar ... the Vietnam War. Many vets returned severely addicted to heroin. However, when they returned to their families, according to the study, over 95% not only overcame the addiction, they stopped cold turkey. [1]

The study has many implications, but for our purposes, we have to understand that connection—meaning the way our kids most need and most understand—is not a luxury. It's not an option. Connection changes everything for our kids. As the research showed, connection is essential to survival. It's a preventative to addiction.

There is no shortage of information on how to

connect with your kids. Social media and family magazines are cluttered with it. But, what there is a shortage of is urgency and the basic understanding of the foundational reasons for it —the significance of it. We know we should connect, but we don't know why.

Moms typically land in the camp of "everything is fine" or "I'm too overwhelmed, I'm giving all I can."

Neither is enough.

The truth is, it's easier to think of work, the grocery list, or getting the car fixed than it is to listen to that same song your toddler loves, again, or to discuss the piece of artwork she made—that we are probably holding upside down anyway, or to tell them every outfit they try on looks amazing. Every stage of a child's life has quirks and things that wear us out. It comes with the territory. We want to find ways to connect to our kids through every stage, but we don't always have the patience and acceptance that make it easy. Most of us have to work at it.

Connection takes energy. We don't always have energy. I have two words for this: Connect anyway.

There are a million ways to connect with a child; in fact there is a list of 25 ways in this chapter. But connection, ultimately, depends on a few moving pieces and factors. These can include the children themselves—how they like to connect, when, under what circumstances, etc. And, it depends on us—how we're doing and if we have the time, energy, and patience needed to slow down.

Do This One Thing For A Year

So, instead of giving you a million things to try, can I give you the one thing that changes relationships over time, and not just with your kid? It's the simple act of presence—non-judgmental, openhearted, hearing and seeing, and loving without demands. If your child is in daycare, be present more with them at night and on the weekends. If your tween is hanging out with friends and you rarely see them, ask them to stay home at some point and be present with them anyway. If your teen is at practice, or in their room, find an entry moment—a situation to be present to them.

Be patient. It just might feel so good to them

that they may push you away. They may be scared you will stop, or that you don't mean it. Stay with it. Give it 365 days. Be there.

My client, the one from the beginning of this chapter, chose presence for a year. It changed her family life. Ultimately, when she went to an appointment with a pediatric specialist, she had gained so much information from spending time with her son that she not only loved her child, she knew him inside and out. She understood him and could clearly explain what was going on at home so the specialists could zero in and help her.

A year later, I received this email:

(My son) began the therapeutic day school. He did wonderfully there, and quickly became one of the favorites in the program ... They diagnosed him as having ADHD, Sensory Processing Disorder, and a general anxiety disorder.

He was screened several times for Autism, and each time the results came back stating that he is not Autistic. He also was given intelligence and aptitude tests. His IQ is 136, which is in the 99th percentile!! He was consistently making progress and meeting his goals, so around mid-September, we started talking about what is best for him. We dropped him down to a half-day at the program. I received information on how to interact with him and set up special education services; this gives him the opportunity to get an extra year of Pre-K through public schools, free of cost.

There was a lag of a month between the program and Kindergarten, and in the time that we were home together, we had a blast! We went to children's museums, science museums, and parks; we played outside a lot; and we had lunch dates. He played T-ball this fall and started Awanas. And he did great in all of these!

So, we went to our return appointment on November 6, and he was accepted into the special education program, and he was placed in a 3-year-old Pre-K classroom. He did wonderfully in his first week. His very first day, a classmate pushed him, and he didn't retaliate, but he used his words and asked the child not to push him! That is HUGE!

His teacher says he is transitioning well from activity to activity, and that he's doing great in class.

Positive Disconnection: When. You. Just. Cannot.

I get it. Often, it's more destructive and frustrating and tiring for us to connect when we have no ability to. It can stoke our anger. It can stoke our guilt. We all know we should listen, talk, ask, but sometimes we cannot give any more to our kids. So we disconnect. Sometimes out of survival and sanity. Then we feel guilty because we know they may not understand or they may take it personally, but we just cannot.

Acknowledging our limits is necessary. Permission granted!

The child(ren) just need to know we'll return and that it's not their fault. We're just clearing our proverbial kitchen from the previous chapter. ;-)

Children can understand that our leaving is not abandoning them. We are modeling how to take care of ourselves when we hit a limit. When they know that we will return, that they are worthy of our return, the connection then becomes a place of safety and love. They will know that we pull away to take care of our needs, instead of taking it out on them. They will know that we think they are important and will find them. They know they are wanted. They know, above all else, that we will return. We must return. We will do whatever we need to do to recharge, and within 30 minutes, come back, look them in the eye, hug them, listen, engage freely, and laugh. One day, they will know it's okay for them to also respect their own limits as well.

Connection ultimately means I want to be with you, enjoy you, give to, and receive from you. It's openness. A gift. A choice. Sometimes we have to try a million things to figure out where we can connect, but it's worth the effort.

Let me offer a few things to try that have worked in the real world.

25 Ways to Connect With Your Kids

1. Take care of yourself first.
2. Listen to them speak while looking in their eyes.
3. Ask questions.
4. Use the phrase "that's interesting" instead of judging them.
5. Laugh together.

6. Apologize.
7. Ask what they know for sure.
8. Acknowledge fears.
9. Physical touch.
10. Join in their fun.
11. Invite them to your fun.
12. Do something new.
13. Do something old.
14. Share culture.
15. Ask them to teach you something.
16. Sit and read.
17. Tell them a positive trait about them.
18. Loud music and dancing.
19. Meet one of their wishes.
20. Think of 10 things you love about them and tell them.
21. Camp outside or inside.
22. Address any current crisis.
23. Share something you learned.
24. Share stories of family.
25. Go fly a kite.

When We Just Want Our Life More Than Connection

As I write this chapter, I am in the midst of watching several single parent acquaintances as they are in the beginning stages of tanking their relationships with their teens. The worst part is that they don't realize it. It's happening in increments, tiny tears that they will not see for a while, but those tiny increments are pulling away at the fabric of connection.

I watch them choose new lovers over their kids, or make the decision to move without seeking agreement from their kids.

Although the most critical time to watch for this is when we're newly single, parents in every stage may create a life apart from their children. I see it in every age group and every situation— married or not. Sometimes moms are signaled because the kids are now teens and "don't need them as much." Parents, understandably wanting to get on with their life, leave the kids sidelined even when they are home.

I have heard, in the past few months: *"If my son doesn't want to move with me, he can live with his father (60 miles away)."* And, *"My girlfriend has a right to be here."* Or, *"He's almost graduating from high school, I need my life. He'll adapt to my new job where I'm traveling three days a week."*

And the kicker, when a teen asked a parent why

she doesn't have dinner with him during the week, the response he received revealed more than just why: *"On Monday nights, I work, and Tuesday is with my boyfriend and Wednesday is my volleyball night. You're here on Friday so what does it matter?"*

There is no X-ray machine that can show a soul that was just told they are not even third priority to a parent. It changes who they are.

We are all struggling to live in a world where our lives matter. We take the reigns so our kid(s) understand how life is going to work (for us), balancing our own needs and wants with theirs. I have felt the sharp cuts of sacrifice when my dreams were tabled so I could homeschool, and the only thing that remained of my life was a weekly coffee shop "field trip" to play chess.

I understand wanting personal time away, and the wish to do my own thing, but here's what I've learned after 17 years: They are okay with letting us go and "doing our thing." They see and understand we have careers. They understand our "night off" once in a while. What they don't understand is where they fit in. When is it their turn?

We are very shortsighted and misguided in many ways as a culture that thrives on busy, fast, more, me, and accomplishment—again, regardless if we're married or not.

I don't know another way to get this point across—other than to write this open letter to all parents. I don't know if it's for you or not, so use it in any way you need to make an impact in your life. All I'll say is this: I prefer to let my son walk away from me when he's done connecting, rather than me walking away from him because I'm too busy.

An Open Letter to Busy Moms (and Dads) About Connection

I get it. You already connected. You already said good morning. You took them to school. You made dinner. They don't want to talk to you anyway. They're busy with friends, with the next social media craze, playing games. I get it.

If you're single, you are moving on in your life— dating, hanging out with people you love spending time with, engaging people who are kind and who make you feel loved. You spent your three minutes talking to your kid—you corrected their behavior today. Your duty is done and now you get to move on with your own life. I get it.

If you have special needs at home, you've advocated, showed up, cleaned up, and you're worn. You need a glass of wine. A maid. A life. I get it.

If you have a toddler at home, you've been chasing yourself silly all day. They've talked non-stop, and they are with you everywhere. You hide in the bathroom for a breathing space. I get it.

If you have tweens at home, you are stuck in the place between letting go and holding on. You see them outgrowing their kid clothes. They have new ideas, a new style, and they are somewhere between don't kiss me in public but still kiss me before I go to bed. This is a tough age to understand. I get it.

If you have teens at home, they have one foot out the door. They don't need you anyway. If they need you beyond car keys and gas money, they tell you—and since they don't, you can move on in your life, your career, your interests. It often feels like we just want them around and they don't want to be around. I get it.

But, I want to tell you that you don't get the luxury of giving up on connecting in any way, shape, or form while they are under your roof. I hear the reasons, the very good personal boundaries, and the intellectual/emotional wants of your own life. I get that your parents didn't do half of what you do for your kids. And that they should be grateful for the stuff, the screens, school...

Let me make this very clear: You are of more worth than your money, of more value than anyone they will interact with today, and of greater significance than anything they could possess. You continue to breathe life into them.

The only problem we have here is that they believe that and you don't. How do I know? If you knew and believed how essential you are to the development of WHO your kid is in the world, you would change. You would rearrange your work schedule and be home for dinner. You would pick them up from daycare and go have an ice cream cone for dinner—just because you missed them. You would ask the teens to go for a ride because they are learning to drive. Or, go play outside or talk to the tweens even though you don't know what to say. You would know learning what to say is worth every minute.

You'd stop bringing home men or women whom you don't truly know, and pay less attention to your love interest than you do them. You'd break up with any person they don't love. Period. If for no other reason than utter trust that they are picking up on something that is not good for you.

You might lay low on work for that first year of infancy so they can bond, watch, soak you in. That first year sets the stage for the rest of their lives. In fact, the first three do, but I'm afraid to push the envelope here.

Understand this. They need you, but they aren't "saying" it in the ways adults say it. They are hungry for you to be in their life, to show them how they are to be treated by others. If you're a mom, by your very actions you are teaching your daughters how to show up in the world. If you have sons, you are training them for the wife they should love. Make your interactions nothing less than amazing.

If you're a dad, you are, by example, training your sons to be men. They will imitate you, follow you, adore you, and respect you. If you have a daughter, you are teaching her what is acceptable to her from her date, her partner, her husband. Make your standards toward her nothing less than adoration.

I do get it. Your job/boyfriend/girlfriend/ spouse all need you. The kids can wait.

They are your icing on your cake, your best accomplishment, and your prized possession.

No, actually, they aren't, and they can't wait. They are not your gold star on your forehead, your best work, and your retirement plan. They are not just home to take up space before they leave for college, or eat you out of house and home, or give you a headache. They are your life.

Let me say it again. **They are your life.**

Let work, friends, sexual partners, addictions, and the next new car be sacrificed or healed.

Our kids are not sacrifices. They are our blood. They carry on our future legacy. We live on because they will carry the story of who we are with them in their cells. They will tell their partners and their kids about us. We can show up in their lives, impact them, enjoy them, treasure and invest in them. Or they will find it somewhere else. I promise.

They will spend their lives looking for love, aching for affirmation, wondering if they are good enough, wishing they understood what they could have done better so they were seen. They will seek it in illegitimate ways, and when we tell our friends, "I don't know what happened, I thought I taught them better," we will be lying at best, and delusional at worst.

They are our responsibility, no, our privilege, to invest in, to watch unfold, be present for, accept as is, and laugh with. There will be no day at work more successful than the day your teen comes to you with a broken heart, after they did everything they could, and wants to talk it through with you, because you have a real connection with them. It's not odd. It's your life together.

Take my challenge. One year of presence, looking in their eyes, playing with them, showing up, learning what makes them laugh, finding out what their favorite food is, their favorite person in school, their toughest situation with a friend. Find out where they come alive, what they would spend $20 on, or what their favorite memory is. One year of discovering what they think about a current event, about love, about home, about you. One year of ridiculous sacrifice of everything not them, and just being there. Not in their face. Not telling them what to do. Just being with them. Just accepting, going with it, and remembering how much kids just want us to join in.

Let's learn from our kids what matters most in life. Connection. Presence. Family. And that to really grow up, you have to be there and not just play house.

Know this: It's a season. A very long season that is too short in the grand scheme of life.

Apology: The Magic Bridge Back To Connection

When we truly try to connect to our kids, we're going to make mistakes—we're going to miss their hearts, lecture instead of listen, and forget what matters most to them. We're going to fumble. And so are they.

What we need most is a bridge back. When we hurt our kids, we need to intentionally address the act. I know most of us didn't grow up with parents apologizing well, if at all. I know that the thought of humbling ourselves to say I'm sorry, for some of us, feels like we've just flipped our lid. But, we have to realize, children and teens understand apology. We have been asking them to master their apology, most likely the entirety of their lives. We ask them to say they're sorry, to forgive, and to mean it. We ask them to take responsibility for their actions and to face their consequences.

But rarely do children get to see how it feels in return, when someone models to them a true, heartfelt apology. I've found amazing things that have happened since I've truly learned to apologize to my son (and FYI, not just him but EVERYONE in my life). And connection is the one true place where most of us can do that. Where we've missed the mark on parenting, missed their hearts, missed seeing them, chosen work over time with them, used screens when we should have been watching them, and on and on. These are all places where we can legitimately offer an apology.

My friend, Dr. Jennifer Thomas, wrote a book with Dr. Gary Chapman called *When Sorry Isn't Enough*. Because we hang out once in a while, she and I have talked at length about the power of applying her principles to children and parents. We discuss the amazing repair that can happen in relationships when solid apologies are offered by parents. We ALSO talk over fruit and nut salads about relationships, ideas, writing, and her TEDx Greensboro talk.

Here are the components of a great apology as found on Jennifer's site: [2]

1. Expressing Regret — "I am sorry."
2. Accepting Responsibility — "I was wrong."
3. Making Restitution — "What can I do to make it right?"
4. Genuinely Repenting — "I will try not to do that again."
5. Requesting Forgiveness — "Will you please forgive me?" [3]

These will only work if you authentically offer them. If you don't mean it, kids will pick up the scent of manipulation before you even start. A word of caution: Don't use these haphazardly. Don't use this list to just get over it. These are powerful tools to use specifically because you want to repair what you broke. It's easier to teach our kids to do this than to actually act on it, but there's nothing more powerful than a real heartfelt apology.

Actions and Acceptance (Always and Forever) Matter MORE than Words

There is nothing that will change disconnection faster than a solid apology backed with action. After the words, let the actions speak. Let us embody our apology and act with integrity toward them. We will find that not only do we model great apologies, but also our children will know how it feels to receive one. They will also know how to respond to a mistake, beyond guilt and shame—apologies trump that. Finally, they will realize they are of great value and worth, because their feelings were considered and when they want to consider another's feelings, they will have the tools. It's an amazing tool for all involved.

As moms we are life bringers, go-getters, and change agents. We are wired to look for ways to take care of, make better, and heal—all things that require changing the current state to something else. We do that. We are really great at that. If there's no food in the house, we get some. If there's a fight going on, we quell it. If something is broken, we fix, toss, or buy another one. We are on top of the game of school, and improving grades, and making sure they eat their vegetables so they grow.

It's all geared toward change.

But there is a powerful place that we easily miss: Acceptance. For most of us, we don't even know what that means or what it looks like. I mean, isn't it a great thing that we push for change and growth and improvement?

Yes.

But not at the expense of connection. Not at the demand of, or push toward perfection. In fact, many of us are looking for balance, perfection, or at least a decluttered desk. So, the thought of acceptance is not only contrary but can be threatening.

One night, when I homeschooled my son, I was on forums trying again to find more information on nutrition, or what mineral was missing, or what tiny clue could turn the ship. I was exhausted and I decided to accept where he was —to accept that if he never got any better, that I would love him regardless, that I would come up with a plan for him, and that he would be who he needs to be in this world.

This didn't mean lowering my standards or not trying to find something to help him. It meant seeing and accepting what is—in all its frustration and fury, its sparkle and shine. He wasn't perfect, but perfection was no longer the marker of health, nor of life. Nor of anything that mattered to me. Being was. Having everything under tight control was no longer my way of operating.

I still struggle mightily with acceptance. It's years later and I am walking that fine line with a high school student with an eye on an Arts university. Mentally, my checklist of volunteering, grades, and leadership consumes my brain. Especially when there is a standard that isn't being met that can be met. Or when grades are below par and when I ask him about it, I hear: "Oh, you just want me to be perfect."

Maybe that's how it comes across. Maybe I'm not clear enough. What I really want, all these years more than anything else, is personal best —which always trumps perfection. Because, we can all accept personal best with no regrets.

Accepting our child connects us to them. Apologizing to them connects after disconnection and models a bridge of hope. Being present for a year promises connection in a way even we can't imagine. We intersect and change their lives through tangible ways that spell LOVE. That is the power of a phenomenal mom.

As we connect, we create memories that shape who they become in the world. Read on to see how we can intentionally influence our family in the everyday, holidays, and ordinary celebrations of life.

:: DIY Coaching Questions:

1. Choose one of the 25 ways to connect with your kid and act on it.
2. Ask yourself when it's most difficult to connect with your kid.
3. If you spend zero time connecting with your kid, spend five minutes today really connecting. Do this every day for a week.

---

[1] http://greatergood.berkeley.edu/article/item/ can_connection_cure_addiction

[2] http://www.drjenniferthomas.com/

[3] Based on *When Sorry Isn't Enough* by Dr. Gary Chapman and Dr. Jennifer Thomas (Chicago: Moody 2013). This book is an update to the authors' *The Five Languages of Apology*.

CHAPTER 8
Practice #6: We Create Powerful Family Memories

For you if you:

- Feel family life is disconnected
- Want to create amazing memories
- Feel the fast pace of life is no longer meaningful

One refrigerator magnet that remained on the fridge for over a decade taught me half of what I know about being a mom. Credited to Josie Bissett, it simply read, *"You never know when you're making a memory."*

Every interaction, each day, week after week builds family life and memories for our kids. For them, childhood will fade to a mish mash of moments from our interactions.

It's important that we find significant ways to make the most of situations where they feel welcomed, a part of, honored, restored, and free to enjoy themselves. This can easily be done through the path of least resistance of fun, tradition and celebration.

Fun: Forging Memories and Love

Here's my theory: Fun is selfless. It's an unexpected back door to connection. Almost the opposite of control, fun levels the playing field and allows kids to teach parents something. In an effortless way, fun bonds parents and children and helps them to relate in different ways. It allows breathing room from good/bad, right/ wrong, and the other judgments children live under. Fun defies expectations. Fun promotes freedom and emotional safety.

Fun forges memories and fosters love.

One afternoon, I joined Jennifer, a close friend, over Nutella lattes in a historic part of town. Discussing each of her boys, whom I happen to know and adore, the conversation focused mainly on her oldest.

"He puts his hand up and tells me to go away. He doesn't want to speak to me. That's so rude. I yell, and it does nothing. But I don't know what else to

do."

I know this family values communication, but, what happens when one turns 16 and communication is done? You can't make someone listen to you.

So, I shifted gears and asked my friend:

"When was the last time you did anything as a family and had fun?"

"Well, I took the younger boys to get fireworks."

"And Stephen?"

"He didn't get to go. He didn't do his chore so he was left out."

"When was the last time you did something fun with him?"

"Well, he's a teen, and he doesn't want to be with me, and we don't really do anything together, but he does want to drive and we do drive together to get his license."

"When was the last time you did that?"

"Two weeks ago."

Two weeks ago was the last fun thing they did together. This is exactly why I'm going to say something that will blow your mind: There are times when fun trumps communication to connect. I'm not saying that I advocate for teens to be disrespectful, nor should they say, "Don't talk to me." But, I am saying they shouldn't have to "earn" fun. Nor should they have it taken away as a punishment.

Believe it or not, there really is such a thing as "fun research" that supports play. The American Academy of Pediatrics (AAP) released a clinical report by Kenneth R. Ginsburg, MD, MSEd, supporting play as, "essential to the healthy development and well-being of our children by contributing to their cognitive, physical, social and emotional health." Play boosts creativity and helps parents create memories for their children. [1]

In short, fun helps them develop and keeps us connected—even to teenagers.
They do want to have fun with their families, but often, they've had so many consequences

for misbehavior, there's no point for them to re-engage. Fun changes all that.

I've spent years getting over myself and learning the concept of fun, letting go, jumping in. To say this is a conscious practice is an understatement for those of us who try to keep it all together. ;-)

But here are truths, the research fleshed out, that I've seen for myself and others who engage regularly in family fun.

11 Effects Fun Has On Kids

1. Connects in a back door way
2. Places everyone on an equal level
3. Finds a way for kids to teach parents
4. Allows parents to see kids completely differently
5. Allows kids to see parents differently
6. Provides laughter
7. Provides a context for unexpected connection
8. Provides a family culture
9. Helps establish trust
10. Helps keep things light instead of intense
11. Helps guests and friends find ways to be included in family (think: board games,

yard football, funny YouTube videos)

After an hour and a half, Jennifer's family found us and we all went for ice cream cones, the boys helping me find the best flavor ever. Once we were all together, Jennifer brought up our topic of fun. I asked her husband what he felt the most important part of family life was and he responded with, *"communication."* Rightly so, he said, *"Without communication, you can't have family."*

It was AWESOME to hear a dad's input. After thanking him, I respectfully disagreed, though, that communication was the most important thing. The boys stopped licking their cones and looked around, halfway smiling.

I told him that fun was the most important thing. He openheartedly asked, *"How so?"*

"Have you ever just had an impasse with your family where all communication was broken down and everyone was in their rooms and there was no more connecting? Well, when those times hit, you know what the back door to reconnection is? After everyone has had a good 30 minutes to cool down, shift into something less intense, less

*in your face, less authoritarian. It can be as
simple as, let's go get something to eat ... let's get
ice cream, like we are now ... let's throw some
hoops outside ... with no HAVING to discuss
anything. Just hanging out a little and having
fun."*

He listened. His wife was smiling. So, I
continued, *"I think that sometimes leveling the
playing field, and letting things go a little and
laughing, reconnects us faster than all the
communicating in the world."*

He never thought of that—many parents don't.
We prize our parenting on motivating our kids,
getting them to be respectful and obedient, and
to make good food choices. We discipline,
coerce, punish, give consequences—they need
to listen to us or else. So they do. And what does
it get them?

More of the same tomorrow.

Yet, "fun research" suggests a way out of the rut
of discipline as a main factor to carving family
life. Play boosts creativity and helps parents
create memories for their children. [2]

And yet, we don't. Fun is markedly missing in modern family life.

According to the University of Michigan's Institute for Social Research, time for fun and play in children's lives (apart from screens), has decreased significantly in the past 30 years. [3] This is disappointing to me. Fun, play, and laughing are not only free, but they change the brain.

In case THAT wasn't enough, there's more research from Dr. Lee Berk, an immunologist at Loma Linda University, linking laughter with the brain's ability to regulate stress hormones (cortisol and epinephrine), as well as anti-bodies and endorphins. Also, a Stanford team, in 2003, found laughter helps the brain regulate dopamine levels, the essential hormone to feeling good. [4]

This shot of science helps bolster and encourage us that laughter and play are not petty or optional. Although we are busy, taking time to unwind and really lose ourselves in what seems "pointless" is actually the key to not only our children's development, but our well-being and immune system as well.

My friend's husband, Jeff, thoughtfully listened to me as I explained all my reasoning, and after a short interchange he asked the boys, "*Do we need more fun?*" They all smiled and nodded.

Jeff finished, "*I think we do a fairly good job with the younger boys, but we need to make time for things with Stephen.*"

I said, "*Stephen, your mom said you're close to getting your license. Is it fun for you to practice driving with them in the car?*"

He smiled and said, "*Yes. And then once I get it, I can take my brothers around.*" Mom and dad smiled on that one.

Before we left, I asked if we could take a family selfie, which apparently was their first one ever. We squeezed in, smiled, laughed, and for 15 seconds forgot about undone chores, yelling, or ignoring each other. We just made a memory.

Sometimes all we need is permission to switch gears, laugh, and follow the smiles in doing something together—be it fun, silly, athletic, or spontaneous. But for some of us, fun takes a back seat to stress, no matter how much we try. For this, we need to have another memory making strategy that appeals to the routine oriented. Let me introduce the importance of traditions.

Traditions: Remembering Who We Are

Family doesn't just happen; we intentionally create it. Crucial to understanding where we belong and where we come from, and knowing that we are not alone, traditions are a key part of family life that keep us rooted and grounded even as the world spins around us. This is true for kids and parents—we all need to come home at different points in the week, or month or year, and be reminded this is who we are, this is what we do.

Every culture invokes traditions. Quincenterra in the Latin community gathers the family of girls turning 15 years old, to celebrate their transition into womanhood. The Jewish community's bar or bat mitzvah initiates girls and boys into man/womanhood. Each and every culture has traditions that keep it alive and vibrant.

Today, many of us are very busy and we don't

create traditions that matter to us. Our modern day hustle makes it easy to forget the traditions we grew up in—to the detriment of building family life.

Syracuse University reviewed 32 publications, published from 1950 onward, where family traditions and rituals were considered. From all the published studies, and over 50 years of research, they found family traditions were foundational for at least four factors. One, they strengthened the family relationships of those involved. Two, they provided a way for people to feel part of a group. Group membership is incredibly powerful. Three, marital unity and satisfaction were much higher when routines and traditions were followed. Finally, adolescents had a significantly higher sense of personal identity than teens from families who did not have practices that bonded them. [5]

Want to know two of the traditions and rituals that did all this?

Family reunions and Sunday dinners.

While not the only events discussed in the studies, these two were the significant traditions that made the impacts discussed above. Imagine the positivity when we factor in holidays and other cultural family points of connection.

The point when creating traditions is not about whether we're doing enough or doing it right. The point is—are we doing it?

There was a season where our family moved several times within a short span of years. Although I would have preferred to find a quiet corner and rock myself for hours on end, days were filled with packing, loading trucks and storage rooms, and figuring out next steps. It was an incredibly stressful and disorienting time as we relocated in and out of several neighborhoods.

However, we still had Survivor Night.

Survivor Night meant that all chores were done before 8pm and we would gather to watch the TV show, Survivor—with homemade, warm, chocolate chip cookies. There were no other rules except to be quiet until the commercial came. Then we gave opinions on who would be voted off and had discussions about values like lying, cheating, and playing a game. Often, my son's friends would come over and join us (mainly for the cookies). It became an unintended tradition that we created.

I never realized how stabilizing it was for nearly 10 years until a year after our final move. We just outgrew it. We skipped a season, and still made cookies on Wednesday night. Then slowly, we skipped more seasons and cookies. Finally, there was more talk about being on Survivor than watching it.

While a fairly random act, it sits firmly in my bank of family memories, of who we are, and what we loved.

Creating Traditions In Your Home

Hopefully, by this point, the creative juices are flowing and you're wondering what tradition you might already have in place. Maybe you want to add something else to your daily, weekly, or monthly routine that might bond family memories and accomplish everything from stronger relationships to personal identity.

Let's start on the paths of least resistance.

What were the traditions you had growing up?
These could be an extended family event, or a
holiday food, or annual gathering.

What helped you connect to extended family in
interesting ways?

With a little planning ahead, which dreamed up
ideas can you commit to this week that might
impact your family?

While you're thinking, let me offer some
traditions you most likely already have in place:

1. Eating with the family most nights
2. Holidays with beloved family and friends
3. Kids' weekend sleepovers with friends

What's most important about traditions is
creating a sense of identity where members of
the whole family safely belong, and where
memories are made. Beyond fun and tradition,
there is one more amazing strategy that singles
out one person for acknowledgement and/or
recognition for something that deserves praise
– the practice of celebration.

Celebration: Creating Personal Memories

Celebrations give us a way to model seeing others, acknowledging something amazing about our families, honoring them in some way that the rest of the world never will. Home is such a place of vulnerability—as moms, we often have to correct and control; we're oftentimes in a hurry. Children (and spouses) can potentially feel disconnected, lost in the shuffle, unacknowledged, or simply unseen. Not loved, and questioning: Do I even matter?

However, with regular points of celebration, we slow the world down and say: You are more important to me than my agenda, my getting things done, and I want to celebrate you—who you are, what you've done, what we've all done as a family.

For a long time in our family, we used a "celebration plate." This larger than normal, bright yellow plate signified someone was special in our home. As the table was being set for dinner, anyone could put the plate at someone else's seat. This signified that person was going to receive compliments, recognition, and acknowledgement for something. Everyone participated, even though it was one person's idea. The only real rule was you couldn't give it to yourself. ;-)

Very often we would give it to someone who looked like they were having a bad day, or stressed. Sometimes we would thank someone for a good deed, or job well done, or great report card. Other times, it was for no reason but just to express love. While everyone was deeply touched, I often felt tears welling when it was my turn, because receiving positive words from my family felt like my entire perspective shifted. Instead of feeling the day was a loss because of anger, I heard I was "brave" or "fun."

More than once, my son's friends were over for dinner and someone issued them the special plate. Often we chose to honor our guest as the person who got bombarded by amazing things that, many times, no one had ever told them before. I think it changes lives. Celebration changes family life.

Let's be moms who set the standard for good at our family table. Be the mom who celebrates. I think we often think this is too minor or too silly, but this changes lives, it connects, it says I see you and I ADORE you.

What if you don't do enough? Do something, and see what happens.

I understand that when things in the house are tight or upsetting or crazy or sad, it's really not on the top of anyone's list to celebrate and think of something good about someone. But, do something.

It's easy to believe that fun, traditions, and celebrations "just happen." But for phenomenal moms, we get to create memories by carving the shape of opportunities through the year. We recognize this will take time and yet, the practice of this yields influence on our children far into their lives. They will remember how they feel and how they were loved. Like a favorite coffee mug says, "We do not remember days. We remember moments. – Caesar Pavese."

:: DIY Coaching Questions:

1. What do you think is fun? Invite your kids along.
2. How can you make existing celebrations even more special?
3. How can you make your own tradition?
4. What can you do on a semi-weekly basis that celebrates a family member?

---

[1] http://www.livestrong.com/article/170399-effects-of-laughter-on-the-human-brain/

[2] http://www.livestrong.com/article/170399-effects-of-laughter-on-the-human-brain/

[3] http://www.livestrong.com/article/170399-effects-of-laughter-on-the-human-brain/

[4] http://www.livestrong.com/article/170399-effects-of-laughter-on-the-human-brain/

[5] http://www.apa.org/pubs/journals/releases/fam-164381.pdf

CHAPTER 9
Practice #7: We Live From Our Spirit

For you if you need:
- Help out of confusion
- Direction for your life or guidance for your children
- Answers, but sanity will do!

Quite possibly, the best spiritual description of motherhood comes from Rachel Cusk, a Canadian novelist, who wrote:

"As it stands, motherhood is a sort of wilderness through which each woman hacks her way, part martyr, part pioneer, a turn of events from which some women derive feelings of heroism while others experience a sense of exile from the world they knew." [1]

From the wilderness, to martyrdom, to victory, to exile, we enter a holy and heroic journey when we become mothers. For each of us, the terms of our soul are forged in fires of 2am feedings or 2am late nights waiting for teens. Over the span of nearly two decades, we find our faith, lose our soul, and rediscover the ways life is bigger than us.

I tread lightly—although our journeys run parallel, our spiritual pilgrimages diverge. Some of us are on a spiritual path, others are watching, and yet others are not sure there is a path, but cheer us on if we think we are on it. Although my perspective is formed through God finding me as a teenager and experiencing every Christian denomination, I extend this chapter to all of us who find the irony of juxtaposition in motherhood, faith, and dear-God-please-help-me.

Motherhood and The Great Disconnect

Many of us would agree that children are a miracle in many ways. Although we sign up to be part of the process, it unfolds without our help, our opinion, or our control. It just doesn't stay that way for long. Our new babies very well may have heaven on their brains when we first meet them. But then they face fear, cold, hunger, and utter helplessness. We rush in to keep them alive, and simultaneously waver between

martyrdom and pioneering a new world, as
Cusk's quote above so aptly describes.

Often the martyring happens to our spirit. We
easily become disconnected from our spirit
through sleep deprivation, feedings, and
profound identity shifting—and our souls skip a
few steps trying to keep up. At some point along
the motherhood journey, we all struggle,
question, wonder. And, in between making
lunches and laying our own head on the pillow,
we ponder if we are in some way disconnected
from our soul.

I think it's safe to say we've all wrestled with the
questions: What if I'm not doing or being
enough spiritually? What if God wants more
from me? How will I even know? Am I teaching
my kids by example?

It's safe to say we grow as moms. We shift,
expand, and accommodate our growing children
so naturally we are also growing. Often, this
means there is a disconnect between where we
were and where we need to be to meet
everyone's changing needs. This typically
happens every few months when the children
are young, and then in cycles and spurts as they

grow.

Spiritual disconnect can be a by-product of all this personal growth. It may feel like everything around us is out of control, and as we grasp for control, we forget our spirituality. We may forget to sort our inner life before reacting to the loud outer life.

Of course we wish we could be the center of calm in the midst of chaos. The beautiful reality, though, is that God is on our back burner for most of our day (and night, for some). Unless we consciously pray throughout the day, we leave filling our spiritual 'cup' till Sundays, or when we can (no judgment) and sip Him (God) as we find time.

So often the upheaval of life throws us into overdrive. We deal with daily schedules and demands like a novice juggling balls. These balls start to drop and then we think we are not enough. But really, we may need spiritual help to make sense of which balls to juggle.

Spiritual disconnect can include things like our relationship to money –spending more than we make, feeling not grateful for what we do have, etc. Another area is our relationship with our kids—is it loving and clear, or based in fear and anger? Are we patient with them, or frustrated and short tempered? Our connection to others may be off. Are we joyful, willing to listen, ego-sacrificing, or feeling unappreciated, ignored, and exiled?

Our relationship to ourselves can be another telltale sign of disconnect—are we seeing our worth only in terms of what we are accomplishing or are we living from our value and calling? While each of these areas can be remedied through solid commitment to change, there is also a spiritual undercurrent in each of them, that when engaged on a spiritual level, changes not only mom's life, but the family's life as well.

Quick Ways to Reconnect To Your Spirit

I'm pretty sure God knows we are both incredibly busy and profoundly in need of reconnecting our spirit to our life. Through the ages, and religious traditions, there are many practices people have relied on to assist them in refocusing on God, and they find that many of their problems seemed to either go away, or they found new perspective or miraculous help.

These are just a few disciplines that go beyond the logic of the physical self, and offer ways for us to look outside of our own, worn out mind for answers and/or help and just a little sanity.

Surrender may be the easiest and most interesting spiritual practice. When we let go and acknowledge we are done, that we have no more tricks up our sleeve, or even if we did, we are too worn to use them—this is surrender.

Prayer includes any words directed to God. This can be "help" or ten minutes of yelling, screaming, crying. It all counts and it all refocuses us away from ourselves.

Reading one passage or verse of a holy book and asking for guidance on applying it helps us to remember we are not alone.

Solitude and silence spans the centuries as a tool for refocusing. Personally, this is my favorite. Admittedly, the quickest way can only happen behind a locked bathroom door and the longest may be an extended weekend away. If you're an introvert on any scale, this is not optional.

Gratitude, although almost so common we ignore it, is scientifically proven over and over to change our happiness levels. Finding one tiny thing—anything—to be grateful for often starts an avalanche of blessings we recognize.

Practicing the presence of God can be adapted to your understanding and concept of God. In essence, it's being aware that God is with you already—no earning it, no needing to pray a certain length of time, no spiritual practice so God shows up. Just acknowledging He's with you during the entire day.

Nature is profoundly healing and we often ignore it. If you live in a big city, don't discount the oxygen swirling around or the water in the sink—even these simple reminders of God's unseen presence in the world restores our soul. Seriously, next time you're stressed, light a candle and run your hands under water for even 60 seconds and see if you experience a moment of peace... your family will think you're washing your hands or doing dishes so this one is beyond perfect. ;-)

Holding prayer beads. I know this may not be your religious tradition, but prayer beads just feel like God is present. Hold one bead at a time and say a prayer for each person in your life, or each obstacle facing you. It's interesting how even two minutes of something out of the ordinary can refocus our spirit.

How Our Spiritual Journey Effects Our Child(ren)

While we truly need the benefits of living a spiritually connected life, sometimes it's easier to think we're good, that we can deal with the craziness on our own. Often we can. But then our children have moms who are not using all the superpowers.

When we're connected spiritually, we interact differently with our kids—we know things. Like, we know when homework wasn't done, or we know we should ask a question about a friend. We see and feel things that come from a higher place. The best way to tell is when others say, *how did you know?*

But even more profoundly, a spiritually connected life benefits the children, because we find and live from a source that's not them. We show up to our family in some way empowered as if on an internal generator inside. We extend love differently and no longer act from as much fear or anger because we've sorted ourselves or received some clarity or instruction from God. We give our time and energy to them differently, because there's no longer anything to prove. We can just be and enjoy them.

Of course, we're no Mother Teresa, trying to wrangle our days, but something on the inside of us changes and we live from the inside out. And not only can our kids tell the difference, but we are living, by example, a life that can be grounded in God in the midst of the daily grind.

The Deep Yes

When we truly find God deeply in our souls, our life uncovers its deep yes.

Being a mom is our life's response to God's calling for us. On some level, we can rest instead of making everything in the world happen. Our spiritual center becomes the loudest voice in the room, and even washing the dishes reveals itself as a holy act.

Honoring our "intuition" or "gut," we align with what is most true and sacred about us in the world. Acknowledging our discontent, engaging in practices that refocus and re-center us, and following the guidance we know, life opens up. Our life, in all its beauty and struggle, becomes the deep yes.

When Our Life Says Yes In Return

Let me give you an example of a mom, Stacey, who wrestled with her life's deep yes. She had a four year old girl and a six month old boy. Many moms feel the weight of the expense of diapers and formula and clothing every few months. If we're married, we want to help our mates provide for the family.

She reasoned that she would go back to work to help out with the family. The one teeny tiny thing that held her back was her son. She said, *"I just wanted to be here for one year for him."* Oddly enough, week after week she couldn't decide if she should go back to work or not, and if so, how and where. She filled out a few applications, but she never put feet to the ground on finding a solid job.

I began suspecting this wasn't about work. I asked, *"Stacey, in your heart of hearts, is working right now in the best interest of your family? Is the thing your family most needs more money?*

What is your spirit most leading you to do? We can take it from there."

She answered, *"In my heart, what I think my family needs is me here. I really just want another six months home. But, I'm worried about money."*

We quickly shifted gears. She chose to take a few steps toward the sacred positioning of her life. She knew. God was already stirring the pot and we just needed to take off the lid and inhale. We had conversations about budgets, saving money, and cutting corners to make ends meet.

Within two weeks, we watched miracles happen. Her student loans got refinanced. Credit card debt got consolidated to manageable payments. Within four months, her husband got another job, moved the family to a simple home that included land, and she is currently working from home. But, she's still home after three years.

This is just one of many examples that fall into place when we listen to our soul—every example is tailored to the person and situation. This is not a story about working or money, or staying home or moving. This is a story about listening and following even when it's gut wrenchingly hard to do so—and trusting that direction will be given, something will come through, and miracles will pop up, because we're living from our deep yes and it's all miracle.

When we are connected to our soul/spirit, we find that all the practices of phenomenal moms we've covered so far find a new sparkle. We use our connection to God to validate our need for care—instead of require our children to meet this need. The talents, abilities, and interests that light our life fulfill some of what we were made to do beyond motherhood. Finding and receiving ideas and a vision for our family comes from a God who knows us intimately and knows what our best, in His eyes, can really look like. Moving past anger and ego, we not only find God's love for us, but renewed love for them.

Creating connections feels more effortless because our soul is grounded and not a vacuum. Our traditions, celebrations, and fun happen more easily because our focus is beyond ourselves and we teach our families where to look. Bottom line—when we practice connecting to our spirit, we model for our family what a spiritual life means—the power of a phenomenal mom. And nowhere else in life is this needed more than in the next practice we'll consider: The one of letting go.

:: DIY Coaching Questions:

1. What faith practice might most help me right now?
2. What do I need to get back to doing, or not doing, to help myself spiritually?
3. Which new faith practice may be something I am open to trying?

---

[1] http://www.brainyquote.com/quotes/keywords/motherhood.html#PVsEu8m6rI1mAHE.99

CHAPTER 10
Practice #8: We Master the Art of Letting Go

For you if you need to:

- Change your relationship to everyone
- Recognize the process of allowing kids to grow up
- Redefine your role as the child(ren) grow

My dear southern-born-and-bred friend, Sharon, is ahead of me in the mom world with two sons in college. She is my go-to when I need help letting go.

In her most comforting drawl, she has often told me, *"Vikki, I'm goin' to tell you something. We all know it. We all know when they hand us our babies—they have an expiration date on them. We know it but we never really get it—until it's here. We know we're supposed to let go, but man. It's not easy."* It may be her accent, but her words always feel like a hug that promises I'm going to get through this.

There is a moment in time where we all realize:
My child is growing up. It's a sinking feeling
where literally every cell in our body shifts and
life flashes forward to high school graduation.
I've seen this moment happen in women when a
child is as small as one year old. Very often it
happens at the end of fourth grade, or during
some "first," like a sleepover. They're on their
own in some way, and they thrive. I'm convinced
there's some spiritual message they send us
that says, "Thanks! I've got this!"

It's tough enough to understand our children
grow up, but I really don't think we understand
their leaving our care in some way, regardless of
their age. In an attempt to let go of my own son,
I started a series on my blog called *#115
Wednesdays*, counting down the weeks until my
son went to college.

I made it to #99. 16 posts and I stopped. Every
time I wrote a blog post, all I wanted to do was
hug him and make him food. And he's only in his
third of four years of high school. I call Sharon. A
lot.

Letting Go: The Challenge

Whether the first day of daycare, nursery school, kindergarten, junior high, or high school, letting go is incredibly displacing. The deep yes of our life revolves around being present, helping, fixing, taking care of, and in every way making sure they stay alive and well.

Here are some words from Eden Hensley Silverstein. She responded to a question about letting go in sending kids to school on The Mom Whisperer Facebook page:

"I don't yet have a Kindergartener, but I remember when I first dropped my little one off at a day care, the advice my mom gave me when she bounded off through the door without a second glance. Her advice was savor their independence—you helped instill it—when they might be able to turn around and see you. If you need to cry, hold the tears until you're out of sight, and then when you see them again, let your face light up at the sight of them. Always let them know how special they are. (My mom said I basically ran into the Kindergarten room without a backwards glance or even a goodbye.)"

I love Eden's story because as a grown woman I

cheer her on. I LOVE her mom for being strong. But, we all know that when mom went home, she cried all the way—her child was no longer as dependent. This is the essence of letting go: supporting independence through our tears.

School becomes an annual marker of growth. The less obvious markers include the first time a child wants to wear what they want to wear. Or, when we realize someone isn't eating all the food on his or her plate because it's not pizza. Or when we hear the words, "You're not the boss of me!" with an accompanying defiant glare. Other possible development cues that a child is ready for more freedom, more independence and self-reliance include disrespect, locking themselves in their room, or announcements of hair color changes. What we often think of as bucking the system or colliding with established rules, might be their way of extricating their life from our apron strings.

Our challenge, when extrication is initiated (always by them, almost never by us), is redefining motherhood and who we now must be for them. We learn to navigate a new purpose —engaging supportively instead of hovering, helping, or hounding. The truth is, we are bound to our children for life. But how tightly we are bound must shift.

Another challenge is letting go of control. Truth be told, we don't want to be that mom who always controls, or is negative, or knows best. Ugh. Sometimes we don't even realize we are doing it. Okay, we NEVER think we're doing it but we probably are. We are all helicopter moms in some teeny tiny way, and if we can own it, we can change it. If the child has earned our trust, we can pull back. Let them spread their wings (at any age). But, it's tough for us to do so.

Our children are our life for a fairly long season of our lives. Letting go feels like a form of grief, losing what was familiar in our interaction with them. So, how can we lean into letting go? I have a few ideas, and they circle back to the first chapters. Figuring out how to let go while staying connected is the quintessential challenge of phenomenal moms.

How To Let Go Like a Pro

Letting go starts in our own mind, heart, and soul. It's almost as if someone needs to signal permission that it really is okay to pull back as much as possible. So here we go: Your life will absolutely shift and change and that's okay, here's why:

You are in the company of many moms who are officially phenomenal.

We actively care for and engage in our own life, and foundationally separate from our children (in the very best way)—we have both connection and independence from them already, and we don't need them to be our stability for life.

Secondly, as we honor our talents, abilities, and interests, we have this to keep us in movement, during their teen years especially. Thirdly, we can lean on our spiritual practices to help us stay grounded, keep perspective, and know everything is on time and fitting into the bigger picture of our lives.

Once we find a place for our own heart and soul to land, we can begin the lifelong process of letting go of them. Life. Long. Process.

Some places to start: If your young child is developmentally ready to dress themselves, make their own breakfast, make their bed, help with chores around the house—if developmentally they can do it, try to teach them and see if they are willing to do it without your help. This counts as supporting their independence.

As they grow, you can look for other signals that you may be more ready than they are: Does it drive you crazy to make their lunch, pack their school backpacks, or put video games away? Most likely you know they can and should be doing all these things for themselves. With a few lessons on how, and expectations expressed, kids starting at age six will be helpful members of the home.

Another place to look is language. Instead of stating our opinion, and saying what "should" happen, we can progressively ask them more and more for their opinion. Instead of blaming, "What were you thinking?" we can ask, "What's the plan?" Pull back and say nothing, or let them figure out how to get out of a jam.

A final but significant place for moms to begin letting go is the area of control. None of us want to be the helicopter mom. Most of us would say we might have a few control issues, but nothing that strains our family life. So all I ask is this one teeny tiny litmus test: Watch during the week to see how many times you have great intentions and seek to "help" but your children never asked.

In fact, just check to see if you jumped in unannounced and in some way took over the task. It's best to just be curious and see how often or not this really happens. Then, there is a better marker for figuring out how much control issues are in place.

Susan came to me for a parenting plan. As the weeks progressed, it became clear that momma bear was struggling to let go. Because her twelve-year-old was not as physically developed as other children his age, she treated him as if he were much younger. This proved difficult for the whole family because of a disconnect in expectations, chores, and behavior.

"He is so small. He is my little boy. So, I baby him. I don't always back my husband when he disciplines, and I go too easy on him." Realizing the problems in the family stemmed from her, she wanted to understand how to begin letting

go. So I told her a story I think of nearly every day...

"Do you know what happens when you cut the cocoon of a butterfly open?"

"No."

"When you cut open the cocoon, you prevent a butterfly's wings from getting stronger. By taking away the struggle you deprive its process of becoming strong. In effect, it's crippled. "

"That's what I'm doing to my son?"

"That's what you're doing to him."

Allowing Our Children To Signal Us

Although most of us will fall into the category of holding on too long, the flip side is letting go too early, or before they've proven they are ready.

Typically, there are two age spans where this happens. The first is when they start school. It's easy to think they want independence but ignore the clingy behavior when they come home from school. Or, the behavior changes because they are not quite ready for their new life apart from home. While the child truly will figure out the new routine, recognizing their reluctance and staying as close as they need is a sign of a phenomenal mom.

The second age span where many moms let go too early is in the teen years. Once they hit high school, parents think, "They just don't need me anymore." So, we work longer hours, or find other ways to get on with our life, all because we've made incorrect assumptions about their life. You may be asking yourself, *Have I done that?* Because it's really hard to tell when you're in the situation if this is happening.

Often, teens with too much freedom have a few telltale signs. They are disrespectful to their parent or to guests. Sometimes they stay away from home because no one is there for them. Some plan to leave home and move in with a friend before finishing high school. They may feel uncared for, not engaged with, and left alone. The family may not know their friends, may not check homework, ask about their day, or forget to enforce a curfew. Assuming teens are more ready to launch than they really are creates a cycle of disengagement that happens long before the final day of senior year.

In his book *Real Boys: Rescuing Our Sons from the Myths of Boyhood*, William Pollack, PhD, eloquently summarizes:

"Boys are pushed to separate from their mother prematurely. Mother is expected to 'cut the apron strings' that tie the son to her and the entire family. As early as age five or six, many boys are pushed out of the family and expected to be independent —in school, camp, at all kinds of activities and situations they may or may not be ready to handle. We give our boys in early adolescence a second shove—into new schools, sports competitions, jobs, dating, travel, and more.

The problem is not that we introduce our boys to the world—that's what parents should be doing —it's how we do it. WE expect them to step outside the family too abruptly, with too little preparation for what lies in store, too little emotional support, not enough opportunity to express their feelings and often with no option of going back or hanging course. WE don't tolerate any stalling or listen to any whining. That's because we believe disconnection is important, even essential, for a boy to 'make the break' and become a man. We do not expect the same of our girls. In fact, if we forced our daughters to disconnect in the same manner as we do boys, with so little help and guidance, we would expect the outcome to be traumatic."

Although this insight centers on boys, there is a point that translates to girls as well: Be aware of the child's inner timetable for letting go. As we discussed above, watch, listen, offer support, and let them sort themselves, without demand or expectation of what's "right." [1]

If this describes your home, there are ways to reconnect and reconfigure life. As the adult, we have to step into leading and influencing our family until they physically leave our home. It's a balancing act—we are looking for ways to let go, yet we are looking for ways to stay present and connected in a supportive way. But it's a balancing act worth steadying.

Letting Go: The Joy

We lived near the home of the late Dr. Maya Angelou. When she passed, her home church celebrated her life with city officials and extended family that were often outside the sphere of media attention. In front of a full church, Dr. Barbee Oakes, Assistant Provost for Diversity and Inclusion at Wake Forest University, spoke of a personal interaction she had with Dr. Angelou when she worked at the university. After explaining to her confidante a problem that she was battling with, including the risks it presented, Dr. Angelou plainly asked her what she was afraid of. She answered, "What if I fail?" and Dr. Angelou said, "Oh, my darlin', what if you fly?"

What if they fly?

What if the more we let go in healthy, appropriate ways, the more our children show us their fluttering wings? Once we trust that fluttering is necessary, brilliant, and beautiful, new ways to let go will present themselves. No doubt, we must resist stepping in to save the day, or "helping" when no one asked us. But this is the practice of the phenomenal mom: encouraging our children to try things on their own, where they will discover that either they fly or they tried. But either way, we will celebrate the transitions of their growth, in their own timeframe, as we hold them with open hands. If not phenomenal, then truly extraordinary. ;-)

Either way, we are carving our legacy on their hearts and souls. How well we prepared, let go, and launched our child(ren) becomes our legacy. May our link in the great chain of generations be informed and ignited by the next chapter.

:: DIY Coaching Questions:

1. Where do I find myself micro-managing, hovering over my kids, or using other forms of control?
2. Do I help when I've not been asked?
3. Do I want to let go?
4. What am I afraid will happen if I let go?
5. Is it okay for my kids to learn?

---

[1] Pollack, William. Real Boys: Rescuing Our Sons from the Myths of Boyhood. New York: Henry Holt and Company, 1998. Intro p. 24.

CHAPTER 11
Practice #9: We Rock Our Legacy

For you if you need:

- Encouragement for every single day
- Ways to understand the past, present, and future of your family
- Powerful perspective on why you matter

Often, being a mom feels profoundly isolating. Whether we work, stay home, are single or married, we often face the sense that we live in our own bubble. Some of us may for a season because our families require more time, energy, or attention from us. But we are far from alone. We are links in a vast chain of ancestors whom I often think may be cheering when they peek down from time to time. From their perspective, we are fulfilling an amazing destiny—one that came before us, and one that we are leaving for those yet to come.

Let's consider our moment in time by the numbers:

Three million years. With a generation being 20 years, that's 150,000 generations behind you.

Here's how the stats play out:

- Probability of boy meeting girl: 1 in 20,000
- Probability of same boy knocking up same girl: 1 in 2000
- Probability of right sperm meeting right egg: 1 in 400 quadrillion
- Probability of every one of your ancestors reproducing successfully: 1 in 1045,000
- Probability of your existing at all: 1 in 102,685,000

As a comparison, the number of atoms in the body of an average male (80kg, 175 pounds) is 1027. The number of atoms making up the earth is about 1050. The number of atoms in the known universe is estimated at 1080.

So what's the probability of your existing? It's the probability of two million people getting together—about the population of San Diego—each to play a game of dice with trillion-sided dice. They each roll the dice, and they all come up with the exact same number—say, 550,343,279,001.

A miracle is an event so unlikely as to be almost impossible. By that definition, I've just shown that you are a miracle.

> *"Now go forth and feel and act like the miracle that you are."*
> — *Ali Benazir*

1

In Defense Of Time, Legacy, and Not Being Alone

Here's my geeky little secret.

I love time. I love the concept of it, how we wrangle it, the limitlessness of it, and my own numbered days. In my 20s, before I had a child, I was profoundly aware of wanting to spend time on a life that deeply mattered—not wanting to waste time on things that ultimately didn't matter on my deathbed. There, I said it: Deathbed. But the operative words were "a life that deeply mattered."

Choosing to carve my days intentionally, I realized how much you could fit into a day or weekend (okay, this is pre-child), but those things needed to matter in some way, and not just fill time. Time in its abundance and limitation was fascinating and forced me to wisely consider my choices.

In spite of "time awareness," burnout has been part of my life. During my early teaching years, I felt burned out. During the infant years, I felt burned out. When I worked part-time and then homeschooled, I felt burned out. We don't always talk burnout when kids are little or there's a crisis because we expect ourselves to rise to the occasion, but it happens. We don't talk about this because we can handle it for a short period of time (even a year or two) as long as it doesn't stay as our new normal.

When we are very aware of our days and choices and how they impact us and our family, we begin to carve a life that really reflects our personal best. Many days feel like default—the same routine and schedule. I'm convinced that it's the micro considerations of the day and the larger considerations of the 1-5-10 year plan that make up the quality of life. We can look back and if not appreciate our decisions, at least understand them. We can minimize regret, understand we did our very best, and that we were consciously creating a life we could be part of.

We build a phenomenal life, day by day, choosing our own self-care, our own talents and abilities, learning how to not freak ourselves out, to get over anger, create a vision and live toward it, connect with our kids, bond with our kids, live from our spirit and learn to overcome control. We shape the quality of our life and the ways we build our family so we can send them into the world as solid human beings—not perfect, but at least with a solid footing and foundation to launch into their own world and ultimately family.

This is legacy: to shape and influence our family with love and wisdom so we send them into the world to carve their own path and make their own mark, while honoring the generations that have gone before them. This is the way we send pieces of ourselves into the future—and it not only matters, it's life giving.

No doubt, we live in the legacy of generations that went before us. Sometimes it's as simple as a certain food baked a certain way on a holiday.

Other times we suffer from unchecked vices that have been passed down one generation after the next, such as alcohol, which leaves its mark even if there is no more drinking.

Legacy is tricky. No one knows what will stick—what stories, what traditions, what pieces of DNA. We don't know. So the best we can do is create the very best choices that honor the past, overcome the vices and failures, and set a strong foundation for the future.

We can find stories, do a little ancestor digging, preserve items that are symbols of overcoming struggle and honor them—teaching our kids how and what to honor, and why it's important. But, all in all, what we are doing is setting a groove, a path, a way of being in the world that most reflects who we are and where we came from.

Although no one knows what our legacy will be, I have a few ways I believe we will influence through legacy. This list can be read twice: First for the legacy we will leave. Secondly, for the legacy we've received.

15 Influences of Legacy

1. By recreating the past (for positive or negative)
2. By recognizing the power of present choices
3. By identifying who we belong to
4. By giving an example of who we are in the world
5. By blessing those who came before us
6. By honoring our children for carrying it ahead of us
7. By recognizing what patterns stop here
8. By not being alone
9. By carrying stories, memories, and lessons as tools to use in our own families
10. By remembering the defeats and drama as a warning to future generations
11. By offering a framework of "this is what we do"
12. By providing a launch pad to boost the next generation skyward
13. By anchoring our life in humility and gratitude for those that survived to have us
14. For clues as to our purpose and direction
15. For borrowing strength and courage when we don't have our own. We can feel

theirs wishing us forward.

It matters. It really does.

I ask moms what they want and, over the course of a few weeks, we get the answer. They think they are solving immediate parenting problems —toddlers amuck become understandable, undiagnosed disorders come into perspective, disconnected teens remain disconnected, but mom learns how to intersect them.

They think they're great moms because they understand their kids. I think they're great moms because they are building legacy.

Legacy is largely not discussed in parenting or family life. It's discussed in business successes, and for people with inheritances, and with pop culture icons, but rarely do we discuss legacy as what we are actively living from that's been handed down to us, and what we are handing down to the next generation.

I don't mean just the positives; I mean the whole shebang. The alcoholism we grew up around is handed down if not addressed. The courage to carve a path different from culture is handed down. The brilliant math gene, and the bent toward depression, are all part of our legacy.

"Carve your name on hearts, not tombstones. A legacy is etched into the minds of others and the stories they share about you."
— Shannon L. Alder
2

It can be the thing that instructs future generations what NOT to do. The mistakes, the poor choices that affect social status, the rogue who left town to never return, the grandmother who drank herself to an early grave.

"Very good, Jason Grace," Notus said. "....you have chosen your own path....You cannot control your parentage, but you can choose your legacy."
— Rick Riordan, The House of Hades
3

Our default legacy is the sum total of what our family was about that we carry with us moving forward into our own families. It's not only the negative and difficult. It's also the strengths, the resourcefulness, the savvy we are also privileged to marinate in for 18 years, or before we leave home.

When we identify what it is for us, and what our family life meant to us, we often become very present to what we are carrying into our current family life. This doesn't necessarily mean it is "bad" or "negative." If we look at everything as teaching us something, we can be more open to the process.

Maybe we don't know how to enjoy our family like we see other moms doing, but we didn't come from a family that valued "enjoying" each other. Or, we struggle with being nurturing, or connected, or communicating, or disciplining.

This is often when moms come to me ... when they can't sort it out for themselves, and the life they imagine is not what they are creating. When I ask what they have tried, it's often exactly what they experienced growing up, and they realize it and need another approach. They need other ways to move because what they are doing isn't "working." It's not having the effect that they know is possible in the world. It's because of that little inner nagging voice that says, "Hey, this could be better," that it truly can be better. We would never think it if we didn't have the ability to create it—yes it may take work, but it's possible and so worth it.

Sometimes that means that we need therapy to move past pain. Sometimes we need coaching to move into our strengths and abilities that may feel like they are sleeping (or nonexistent). But very often, just recognizing that we need a new set of tools to parent—or live, or dream a little bigger—is all that's needed.

What's Your Default?

Let's talk about finding out your current place of default. Make a list of how you felt in your home when you were around the ages of seven and 15. List the "negative" things you felt as well as the positive. List memories that highlight those years that back up the feelings. This is often a great start to understanding what you currently bring to the table. If you have a husband who is at home and can do the same thing, it will bring even more light to the dynamic currently going on in your home. Pay special attention to the words that are similar for you both.

Also, this list may be very similar to how your children feel, which is why their actions are the way they are, and why you know more is possible as their mom.

Once you have the list, ask your child(ren) how they sometimes feel at home (whatever they come up with counts: good, bad, positive and negative). Ask them when and why. Children sometimes really do come with their own instructions.

Let me strongly add this warning to this exercise: If your children don't currently feel safe around you, then they may not answer honestly. If you find this to be the case, I strongly recommend personal counseling to learn to move in a different, safer way in your home.

If they do answer, and you listen with interest and thank them, you've just opened up a connection that has the potential to change the legacy you're passing down. Why? Because all children want to be heard, to matter, to have their opinions validated, understood, and honored. They want to be noticed and called out on their brilliance, and respected for their contribution. The last thing they want is to be dismissed for their ignorance, or passed over for their age.

When we come to them, in our own curiosity and vulnerability, we begin to build a bridge toward them instead of demanding that they always understand us. We offer something of humility and kindness when we act in a way that says that they matter so much we are willing to engage with them on their level, hear them in the places that most matter, and accept their answers, whether we approve of them or not.

This one exercise changes our legacy by defining the automatic default to one of intentional crafting. It changes the dynamic of the family lineage in one generation.

When we think of legacy, we think of our grandparents. Okay, and the money they did or didn't leave us. But can we rethink what legacy is?

I have an idea that legacy is a sweet spot of several factors: Our character over time, what is important to us lived out day after day (the congruency of our beliefs), the impact we have on others (how we make them feel), and the truth mixed with exaggeration of perspective.

To break it down into pieces that we can relate to, let me use my own example of grandparents I'm very proud of. I have several grandparents that have given me a legacy of courage, hard work, and love for family.

My father's parents came to the US from Germany after surviving a holocaust in the Ukraine, working on German occupied farms, in Belgian coal mines and prison, and ultimately rebuilding Germany and relocating to the States. Their tireless work ethic, survival instincts, deep reverent spiritual base, and street smarts allowed them to create a peaceful life.

My mother's parents were both born in the US into immigrant families from Eastern Europe. Their joyful, simple way of life, combined with brutally difficult physical work, set the stage for their work ethic, love, and celebration, mixed with a commitment to family and church.

Here's the kicker: This informs me of what's important in raising my son. This is part of what I most understand and have lived. So, when I parent with intention, my legacy is very close to me.

Family
Love
Hard work
Courage
Multicultural understanding
Faith

Why? Because I want my son propped up on my shoulders, as I was on the shoulders of my parents and grandparents.

Immediate Legacy: The Secret of Plus 10

What we most need to consider is who our children are, combined with a dose of guidance and boundaries. Answering these questions is what it means to create an intentional legacy instead of defaulting to our family's history of abusive or addictive patterns.

We don't have four year olds; we have future 14 year olds.

We don't have 10 year olds; we have future 20 year olds.

Who do we want them to be in the world?

When we recognize the power of present choices and decide to make healthy, healing ones, we change the legacy handed to us.

When we identify the strength and beauty of our ancestors and use positive traits to build our current life, we honor the legacy.

When we understand our children will carry our choices and patterns forward so we choose wise, loving and healing patterns, we shift the shape of the legacy we were handed.

When we carry stories, memories, and lessons from our ancestors and grandparents, as lessons and tools to teach our children, we create a different legacy.

By heeding the warnings given to us through stories of previous generations—their faults, failures, shortcomings, we have a lens to consider our own choices and course correct the legacy left to our care.

By recognizing, celebrating, and talking about the family strengths, wins, and "this is who we are" scenarios, we ingrain in our children pride, connection, and a secure place in our family line.

The creation of an intentional legacy that we hand down to our children, inspires us to keep going ... My grandmother, who lived with stage 2-4 cancer for four years, to the age of 96. The grandfathers, who survived wars, and the great greats, who serendipitously knew the hand of God in some way leading, guiding to safety, to love, or to a new world.

We will also be remembered for our story—the days we invested in family.

We are carving that kind of impact.

We may not be making huge feats of daring or surviving great turmoil (or maybe we are). But the steady day in and day out is to not to be underestimated in its impact. The choices we make to love our spouses or leave to save our sanity, these are stories being formed every day of our lives. That's legacy.

So my grandmother said to my mom a week before she died that she was leaving nothing to her grandchildren ... She meant in terms of money. My mom answered with the truth that I would have given were I there. She said, "*Are you kidding? You've given them a lifetime of love and that's better than money. That's more valuable than any money.*"

There was nothing more that needed to be said.

At her funeral, cousins and aunts came up to me and said how she was their favorite. She made them feel welcome. She always paid attention to them. She loved them. I haven't been to a lot of funerals, but I don't always tell people they are my favorite. My grandmother had, over years, carved a legacy—along with my grandfather— of love, of family, of joy.

Death is inevitable. Life—one that really matters, that influences and impacts our legacy and makes a dent in the world—isn't always so inevitable. It takes awareness, conscious creating, and believing that we are never ever alone.

"Everyone must leave something behind when he dies," my grandfather said. A child or a book or a painting or a house or a wall built or a pair of shoes made. Or a garden planted. Something your hand touched in some way so your soul has

somewhere to go when you die, and when people look at that tree or that flower you planted, you're there.

"It doesn't matter what you do," he said, "so long as you change something from the way it was before you touched it into something that's like you after you take your hands away. The difference between the man who just cuts lawns and a real gardener is in the touching," he said.

"The lawn-cutter might just as well not have been there at all; the gardener will be there a lifetime."
— Ray Bradbury, Fahrenheit 451

4

We have to understand we are imprinting ourselves in the lives of our children for their lives. We are gardeners of a very irreplaceable, phenomenal kind.

:: DIY Coaching Questions:

1. Who were my grandparents in the world?
2. Who do I want to show my child(ren) I am?
3. What do I want my child(ren) to carry on?

---

[1] http://blogs.law.harvard.edu/abinazir/2011/06/15/what-are-chances-you-would-be-born/

[2] www.goodreads.com/author/show/1391130.Shannon_L_Alder

[3] www.goodreads.com/work/quotes/21539506

[4] www.goodreads.com/author/show/1630.Ray_Bradbury

CHAPTER 12
You've Got This

There you have it.

The nine ways moms can quickly, and profoundly, impact their family life.

If you are here and feel that more than one chapter applied to you, then I bet you're overwhelmed because you have a life and how the heck are you supposed to make ALL these changes?

I bet that you ARE wanting to change but crap—now what?

Before you make any changes, whip your family into shape (which this is so not about anyway), or even decide what needs to change, please know this first.

You are irreplaceable to them.

You are the sun to their rotating planets and irregular orbits.

For your little ones, you embody who God is. For your older ones, you are modeling pieces of who they are to become. For your teens, you are their solid ground as they flutter their wings.

And all this before you even get out of bed on any given morning.

Who you are is enough for them.

Who you are is all they know for a parent. They are not comparing you. They are not wishing you were better. They are not going to mutiny because you didn't take care of yourself, live in your vision, or intentionally create a legacy for them.

They love you as is.

Here's the flip side.

They are profoundly at our mercy. They are at the other end of our mood swings, and good days. They are at the other end of our yelling, our stress, and our fears.

What I most want us to understand above all

else is that because they are so incredibly dependent on us emotionally, physically, spiritually, etc., they deserve unconditional love, your strength and goodness, and your understanding of their dependence without taking advantage of it (because we have stress or a bad day, etc.).

It's this love, this vulnerability, and their utter dependence on you that motivates change.

Their vulnerability towards us should motivate us to offer extreme love in the way they most understand. This book is basically nine ways to their heart, ways that we can affect by changing ourselves.

Let me give you this analogy: Growing our family with children is like the experience of welcoming a puppy. Please consider the progression of relationships and understand I'm not comparing our kids to dogs, just our relationship to a lifetime commitment of those at our mercy...

A friend calls and tells us we get the pick of the litter from her puppies. She can't keep them, so if we want to have first dibs, it's ours.

It's perfect timing—we were just talking about maybe getting a dog. We have dreams of a dog growing up with our family. We can do bark parks and teach it tricks. It's everything we've always wanted and we haven't even met it yet. We call the friend and we go to choose.

Eight puppies need homes. We overlook the runts, the ones sleeping, and the ones jumping too high or with too much energy. We choose a puppy that was second in the litter—bright eyes, seems to smile, and above all else, runs to us.

Sold.

We name it Bear, take it home to bowls, a bed, a small crate, and know it will be the first of many long nights and clean ups, but we LOVE this puppy. Totally worth it.

Weeks go by. There is great care to take care of it (often around the clock), and training it, and developing a rapport with it. Our friends and neighbors come and play with it. We walk it.

Months go by; Bear is now not so cute. We no

longer coddle and pay attention to it. Walks are maybe once a week—although we know we should do better, we just don't have time. We will go to the bark park, but maybe when it's older.

Saturdays are spent catching up from the week. Bear wonders what has happened and starts to form habits that gain attention—bad habits. Finding leather sandals to chew on, ripping up underwear or towels left on the floor, reverting to peeing in the house. We are beside ourselves and livid.

Puppies grow quickly—within two years, they know better, do better, and respond to us better.

If at any time (especially in the first weeks) we don't take it outside regularly or feed it, and we let others deal with it or ignore it, Bear learns to distrust us. It learns it's not safe. It either becomes aggressive or shuts down and becomes despondent. Either way, it's not the puppy we brought home.

We don't understand or like this new stage.

We know if we let things continue like this, the

dog will run the house. But, to change will take everyone's involvement, new strategies, and a change in routine and schedule. Mom knows it will be on her mostly.

She makes a really hard call.

In fact, she makes one of the toughest calls a mom can make.

She decides to recall the reasons the family decided to get a dog—why they really wanted it, what everyone promised, and long term what it would mean for memories of childhood and this season of their lives. She was sure these things weren't accomplished yet.

The question was, did the whole family still want this or was reality too much? Did they want to find the dog a new home or a family who would love him? A family who would take care of him? Or could they recommit to Bear?

After a long discussion on what it would take, everyone made a tough decision.

They wanted to keep the dog.

They would alter the home routine, enlist the kids to walk the dog, go to obedience classes and ask for help.

In the weeks to come, Mom would remind the kids of their decision and their commitment, and that the dog hasn't been walked in two days. They would take time as a family on Saturdays, apart from friends, to take the dog to the bark park. They would throw a ball after school, hug it, give it attention, and buy it a crate so it had a home it loved.

Over time, the dog learned how to be part of the family. That it couldn't just pee in the house without consequences, that it couldn't tear up sandals or clothing. But it also felt loved—time, attention, and bones and treats.

Bear learns to walk, heel, shake hands on command, go to his crate, and watch TV with the family. Instinctively, he even began to guard the house and bark when strangers were near the yard.

Within a few years, no one even remembered the "sacrifices" of time and routine. The dog was long considered part of the family. The family, now with tweens and teens, forgot how shaped they were by their commitment to Bear and now find it an everyday practice to think of others, decide if a sacrifice is worth it, and log in family time.

This is so with our kids. I'm not comparing kids to dogs but, again, only to the same progression of relationship building, living life, breaking trust, making tough decisions and, eventually, finding training. We know we're signing up for a role we want, we know we don't understand how it will affect our lives. We're often unprepared to know how to deal with results, and we're having to change, make sacrifices, and transform, not just because it's required of us, but because we wanted this different life. We imagined an amazing life different than what we had. We just didn't realize it would come at the cost of the life we knew.

Every dream, vision, and relationship we really want comes at a cost of the life we currently know. And that's not bad. That's not a deal breaker.

That's a gift.

When we become moms, we don't have the option to NOT change. If nothing else, we can't run out for donuts at 10:30pm with our spouse any more. We can't sleep in on Saturdays, at least not until the teen years. Then in the teen years, we can sleep in, but we worry where our kid was last night.

There's no option to stay the same. We change, shift, accommodate, and above all else, face personal growth.

Here are the truths I've discovered and you probably already know:

- Being a mom is personal growth on steroids.
- Personal growth comes with the territory.
- We face stuff we didn't see before. Stuff we don't want to see.
- Ways that we need to grow up.
- Ways we don't want to grow up but apparently need to.

I recognize and honor the courage it takes to take an honest look at your family and say, "This isn't working and I'm going to change it."

And in so doing, you change yourself.

But There Are Things We Will Have To Face

Once our perspective changes, there's really nothing that holds us back.

But there are things we will have to face:

Noticing the ways we martyr ourselves instead of taking care of ourselves.

Leveraging our strengths (what they are, why we didn't do it sooner, facing the shifts).

Semi-confidently trying to seek a new vision, one where our highest hopes for our family are given attention.

Courageously figuring out where we are seeing through our ego, versus where we shift perspectives so we become women of power instead of anger.

Finding our center of vulnerability and risking deep connection with those around us.

Taking time to bond, learn, and grow together with our kids.

Seeking how faith plays a part in our lives or not.

Discovering every day as a link in a long chain of legacy—with us as the center of all that was our ancestry and all that will be our legacy.

The hope is that every day we can all wake up into a new way of being in our family on a day-to-day basis.

Yes they will ask, rebel, test you, and doubt anything new you introduce.

Change is tough for them. It will be tough for you.

But hopefully, once you get to this point, you'll see where you're heading if you don't make a change.

You now see that if you allow a four year old to disrespect you now, you'll have the sassy 14-year-old that no one wants to be around (and who, most likely, will be miserable herself).

You now understand that if you have a son in

junior high who is lethargic and indulges in video games, when he gets to high school, his brain will function very differently than if he explored the world in 3D.

You realize that if you have a teen who refuses to take direction and is rebellious, you'll be disconnected from a young adult who goes off to college and faces life unprepared.

These are some guesses from clients and friends and people in my periphery that I've watched over time. It just never fails.

But here's what also never fails.

The mom who addresses the issue of screen time limits with her 10 year old and has a teen that understands when it's appropriate to text on the iPhone and when it's enough for the day.

The mom who dreamed of a different life for her young children and, instead of a lifeless summer, used weekends to go to the library, free concerts, and art galleries.

The mom who saw her 12 year old daughter's desire to be an interior designer and watched her six years later apply to a top rated school for it in their state, and as if by divine intervention, the funds appeared.

My own son, Jordan, who has a final step to take that is without me and must be without me, to leave home.

Far from perfect, I wish for many moments (not entire days) that I could rewind and have a do-over.

I go to bed every night knowing I did everything I could think of.

He absolutely will have lessons that he needs to learn that I didn't teach.

He may tank, falter, question, and go to a few parties I will not know about until he's 30 with kids. But his life will not only be his own, I know I will have given him the best launch possible.

So as I stand at this precipice, I join you in knowing this:

It's not only possible to have a phenomenal family, but that it's truly just a few decisions and tweaks away.

You have all the tools.

Start. Start with finding just one of the nine for the next two weeks. Try new things. Take steps in a different direction. Believe you can change anything in your home.

Remember this as you try: *You're not alone.* I'm on all social media using these exact nine points as the basis for everything I'm about.

- Join the conversation at www.Facebook.com/TheMomWhisperer;
- Send me first day of school pictures at www.Instagram.com/TheMomWhisperer; tweet me your questions @momwhisperer;
- And find inspiration on the blog, www.themomwhisperer.com/blog.

Go to www.themomwhisperer.com/courses for current class offerings, and www.themomwhisperer.com/coaching for group coaching. Contact me if you're pulling out your hair because you did what I suggested and everything fell apart (which is par for the course right before it all comes together).

Yes, you've got this.

Yes, it's all worth it.

Yes, you really are the most amazing mom your family will ever have.

You really are building a legacy that will outlive you.

You truly are their connection point in a crazy world.

You are their go-to even if it feels like you're the last person on the planet they want to see, except for dinner.

You are teaching your daughter(s) how to have power and vision.

You are teaching your son(s) how to engage with influence in family life.

You embody what their spiritual life could look like.

You set the tone for fun, celebration, and tradition for the rest of their lives. When they grow up and have kids, your example is front and center.

You will not only have addressed and changed yourself, but you will have impacted your children (whatever their ages are—it's never too late). They will grow up knowing a different world than you did, and they will have tools and strategies that you never had—because you stretched outside of yourself and made shifts, answered a different call to hope, and wanted more in life than what you knew (and not just monetarily).

All the struggle you have now will allow future generations the higher ground to see more, better, different, deeper things to wrestle with. But they will have seen you overcome and they will know that whatever they face, it will be worth it.

I wish I could be there and tell you how amazing you are, how many resources are in you already that you can pull from, and how to trust yourself to move toward the changes you seek and the life you dream of with your kids. I wish I could tell you to believe that everyday you are carving, creating, and profoundly upholding not only your life but also theirs—which is why the burden feels so heavy at times.

Your life is more than your life when you have kids. Everything you do, say, think, and act is absorbed. They either take it or leave it and what they take and what they leave is all a mystery. So bringing your best, not every day because we just can't, but in spurts, with intention to show up well and kindly and with sanity, will change not only you, but them.

Choose a chapter for a week or a month. Lean in. Find new footing. Believe with everything you are meant to be that you are doing your dead level best and when you know more, you do more. But for now, you just learned a ton. Take it slow, get support as you need it, believe there is more than what you see going on—and that you truly are affecting it even when you feel like everything else has more influence than you. It doesn't. Hold your ground. Show up. Find yourself. Love yourself with deep compassion and gratitude for your life up until this point. Don't believe that you've failed. You've arrived. And you'll keep arriving and showing up because your life is worth it.

We always have ideas about motherhood.

Mostly, that our family must be awesome most of the time and everything after that means we're failing. And we should feel guilty. And we should worry that they will not make their way in the world. And if we're not guilty or worried, then we've missed something, or some combination of all of the above—depending on the day, the weather, and if there's chocolate in the house or not.

In the spirit of putting things where they belong (beyond the laundry, groceries and mismatched socks), let's consider a few things that motherhood really means and what it does not.

What Motherhood Isn't

Motherhood isn't an attempt at perfection. For every day that we completely surprised ourselves and took care of the bills, didn't yell, made dinner, AND had leftovers for later in the week—is a counterbalanced day of insanity and stress, one where time feels like it's on fast forward and we will miss our 11pm bedtime. Again.

Motherhood isn't the place to prove how awesome we really are. One minute we're being hugged and thanked and within 45 minutes, something has gone wrong and we are trying to either a) fix it, b) find it, or c) clean it. If we have teens, we are trying to not ask ourselves what we did wrong that they are still in their room. Most days we would say we are not awesome and can prove it by asking a family member at any given moment.

Motherhood isn't raising an ideal child. We can't mark our sacrifice by how our kids are in the world. **Yes,** we influence, and **yes,** we have responsibility to teach. But they have this really annoying freedom called "choices" and this other really uncontrollable factor called "nature" (who they are meant to be in the world). Basically, if we aren't ideal people and have faults along with sparkling moments, they too will not be ideal people, and will have faults and sparkling moments too.

One motherhood definition that I've come to bank on daily is that somewhere in the grand scheme of life, we pulled the card that said motherhood is the ***willingness to learn love in a completely different way through change and growth.*** I am willing to be stretched in every way a human can be stretched, while learning to see myself and my child(ren) in a fluid and expanding way. If learning love through growth and resilience can redefine motherhood, then we might define ourselves not only as phenomenal but as Freaking. Awesome. No chocolate needed.

One of the most inspiring poems I've let sink into my life is from Marianne Williamson. I want to leave you with her amazing version, and then my inspired version for moms.

"Our deepest fear is not that we are inadequate.
Our deepest fear is that we are powerful beyond measure.
It is our light, not our darkness, that most frightens us.
We ask ourselves, who am I to be brilliant, gorgeous, talented, and fabulous?
Actually, who are you not to be?
You are a child of God.
Your playing small doesn't serve the world.
There's nothing enlightened about shrinking so that other people won't feel insecure around you.
We are all meant to shine, as children do.
We are born to make manifest the glory of God

that is within us.
It's not just in some of us, it's in everyone.
And as we let our own light shine, we
unconsciously give other people permission to do
the same.
As we are liberated from our own fear, our
presence automatically liberates others."

— Marianne Williamson from her book
Reflections on the Principles of 'A Course in
Miracles.'

I want you to take a minute, because we are
going to work some mom whispering on that
quote. Let it land and sink into the truth of your
own life.

Here's my spin for us....

"Our deepest fear is not that we live in a
cluttered house, or that we can't figure out how
to connect to our kids, or that we can't juggle our
busy lives.
Our deepest fear is that we are more capable,
brilliant, and confidant than we ever thought.
It is our light showing up as our hope, our
perspective, our dreams, not our darkness in fear,
anxiety or anger, that most frightens us.

We ask ourselves, 'Who am I to rock
parenting, enjoy abundant health, pull out my
guitar or artist palette or dreams for a business,
or wear a black dress and go dancing?'
Actually, who are you not to?
You are a child of God.
Your numbing out, accepting less from
yourself, or disengaging, doesn't serve your
family, or their impact in the world—or yours.
There's nothing enlightened about choosing to
be ignorant of parenting, not confronting in love,
or not holding others accountable for their
actions so that they won't feel insecure,
temporarily 'hate you,' or want to avoid you.
We are all meant to shine as moms, just as we
want our children to.
We are born to make manifest the glory of God
that is within us.
It's not just in some moms, it's in all of us.
And as we let our own light shine, we
unconsciously give our children, our partners, our
friends, permission to do the same.
As we are liberated from our own fear of not
being enough or doing enough, our presence
automatically liberates others to know and
believe they are and do enough."

— Mom Whispered® Version of Marianne

Williamson's quote.

When we practice this, we become phenomenal.

Be you.

It's who they most need.

About the Author

Vikki Spencer inspires women from every stage in motherhood to be their best. Her emphasis is on creating lives and families that flow with passion and purpose. Through her own experience helping her child overcome OCD and Tourette's, she understands the fight against guilt to care for oneself amidst crisis and care giving.

In her writing and coaching, she calls women to

utilize their emotional, mental, and spiritual resources to learn about themselves and their "wiring" — and then to care for and influence their families.

Vikki has a master's degree in Education, taught high school, trained by the Institute for Life Coach Training and is a certified Elite Life Coach. She appears on local news, and has contributed to numerous books for moms, including one on post-partum depression.

Can you help?

If you liked this book and it was helpful to you, could you PLEASE leave a review on Amazon? Simply visit http://bit.ly/momifesto to leave your honest feedback!

Reviews are really important to the success of a book—so if you like (or don't like!) what you've read, PLEASE take 2 minutes to leave your honest review —I really appreciate it.

Made in the USA
Lexington, KY
20 July 2015